PETER THE GREAT

The Reformer-Tsar

Sweden
Finland
Karelia
Lesnoy
WHITE SEA
Archangel
URAL MTS.
Olonets
L. Ladoga
Nystadt
Kronstadt
Schlüsselburg
Narva
St. Petersburg
Reval
Ingria
Novgorod
Estonia
Dorpat
Pskov
BALTIC SEA
Riga
Russia
Preobrazhenskoye
Moscow
Libau
Smolensk
Kaluga
Volga R.
Königsberg
Prussia
Mohilev
Briansk
Voronezh
Thorn
Warsaw
Poland
Ukraine
Kiev
Dnieper R.
Poltava
Don R.
Astrakhan
Rostov
Azov
Vienna
Austria
Dniester R.
CASPIAN SEA
Stralsund
England
London
Zaandam
Amsterdam
Hanover
Holland
Belgium
Liège
France
Straits of Kerch
BLACK SEA
CAUCASUS MTS.
Ottoman Empire

IMMORTALS OF HISTORY

PETER THE GREAT

The Reformer-Tsar

by Douglas Liversidge

FRANKLIN WATTS
LONDON · NEW YORK

Franklin Watts Limited
18 Grosvenor Street
London W1

Cover photo courtesy
The Bettmann Archive

Map by Dyno Lowenstein

SBN 85166 295 1

Printed in Great Britain by
Lewis Reprints Limited, Port Talbot, Glamorgan

CONTENTS

CONTENTS

PETER THE GREAT

The Reformer-Tsar

1

THE COURT FACTIONS

In the late seventeenth century, the vast and backward nation of Russia entered a period of sharp reform. Foreigners, who dominated the export trade and commanded the Russian soldiers, brought Western knowledge into the long-isolated Russian nation. Although many Russians clung fanatically to the past, others, including the powerful nobles known as the boyars, realized that the country was ready for change. All it needed was a leader.

On June 11, 1672, that leader was born. History would know him as Peter the Great.

Peter was the fourteenth child of Tsar Alexis, second monarch of the house of Romanov. The Tsar was pleased that the boy was healthy. Three of his sons had died in childhood. Feodor, his eldest and heir, was sickly, and weak-minded Ivan was almost blind.

Tsar Alexis had been married twice, both times to daughters of influential Russian families. His first wife was Maria Miloslavsky, mother of Feodor and Ivan. The Miloslavskys, although not always sincere, fought to keep traditional ways. Peter's mother, the Tsar's second wife, was Natalia Naryshkin. Her family championed the cause of reform because they believed it would be profitable to them.

Peter spent his first years in an atmosphere of turmoil. His father was urged by his wife Natalia's legal guardian, Artemon Matveyev, to bring about reforms, but the pious Tsar lacked the strength to impose them. Matveyev encouraged visitors from the West and tried to create new conditions in which Western ideas could grow. Perhaps because of this contact with Westerners, young Peter developed a deep affinity for Western ideas and a repugnance for the old traditions that had long retarded Russia.

When Peter was four years old, his father died. The boy was soon deep in the center of court intrigue. Although Peter's stepbrother Feodor was the lawful heir, Matveyev tried unsuccessfully to put Peter on the throne. For this hasty and ill-conceived act, Matveyev was banished from the court. He did not return till some years later.

In 1682, when Feodor died childless, Peter was proclaimed Tsar. He was ten years old. His mother was named regent. However, the new Tsar's reign was short-lived, for the Miloslavskys stirred up trouble and touched off a riot. The result was an agreement under which Russia would have two tsars—Peter and his stepbrother Ivan. His stepsister Sophia was proclaimed regent; the two young tsars became little more than puppets.

Peter's education covered a range of subjects. When he was five, he was tutored in religion and the alphabet. He never learned to write or spell properly, but from picture books in the palace library, he did develop a fondness for Russian history. Although he was not a scholar, he had a passion for practical things. At Preobrazhenskoye, a small Romanov estate near Moscow, where his mother had gone after Feodor's death, Peter became skilled in such crafts as carpentry and masonry, and was taught the blacksmith's trade. When he was thirteen, he and some companions built a fortress on the banks of the Yauza River. At sixteen, he learned geography and simple arithmetic, the techniques of fortification and boat building. He never lost his enthusiasm for boat building or for war games.

Having never cared for life at the Kremlin, the governing center in Moscow, Peter was content to remain with his mother in the country. Nearby was a community known as the foreign quarter, where people from various parts of Europe lived. The quarter showed the young monarch how far Russia lagged behind the Western nations, and how much he needed to learn.

Sophia was delighted to have Peter away from Moscow. She was intent on keeping her line, the Miloslavskys, on the throne, and so she arranged a marriage for Ivan, hoping that there would soon be an heir. There was, and when the child was born, the rival Naryshkin family persuaded Peter's mother to find a wife for him. Natalia selected Eudoxia Lopukhin, an attractive girl of noble birth. Peter was not too delighted with the marriage, especially because it interrupted his boat building on Lake Periaslov, some fifty miles north of Moscow. However, it did not interrupt it for long, for soon after the marriage, he left his bride at home and returned to the lake. The following year, his son and heir, Alexis, was born.

But the feud between the two opposing families continued, and the Naryshkins finally persuaded Peter to assert himself at the Kremlin. He was now sixteen years old and six feet eight inches tall.

Peter returned to Moscow and began to oppose Sophia openly, and she made plans to destroy him. In August, 1689, he was warned of an attack by the streltsy, the palace guard, who were loyal to Sophia. Panic-stricken, he fled to a nearby wood. The imaginative and highly strung young man wept openly. The facial convulsions that reflected his terror were to reappear at moments of stress throughout his life.

Although Peter was unharmed, the hostilities were now out in the open. Either Sophia or Peter must leave the Kremlin. At Preobrazhenskoye, Peter had formed a group of aristocrats, grooms, and youths of low birth into two battalions for his war games. This was the nucleus that would one day grow into the Imperial Guard. Now these battalions joined him at the monastery-fortress of Troitskaya, some forty miles from Moscow, along with his mother and foreign officers. Sophia's followers deserted her, and shortly after she was sentenced for life to a convent cell.

Peter was now in power, but he did not wish to banish Ivan from the throne. Caring little for ceremonial affairs, he wanted to have someone available for these occasions. He wrote: "Now, Lord Brother, the time has come when we should rule the Empire as God ordained . . . and as for that third shameful person our sister, be it thy will, my Lord Brother, she shall no longer arrogate the title. It is shameful, that now we are both of age she should independently of us possess the State. I declare to thee my wish and beseech permission . . . to name just judges and replace those not fitted, so giving quickly peace and joy to the country. And when we are together, Lord Brother, we will put everything in order and I shall be ready to honor you as I would my father."

For a while Ivan remained on the throne as a figurehead, attending to functions that Peter disliked. But eventually Ivan retired to the peace of a monastery. Peter was the sole power of the empire. A chapter in the story of Russia had closed; a more momentous chapter was about to begin.

2

WAR: SHAM AND REAL

Although Peter would one day be called "the Great," at this period in his life there was nothing to indicate that he would mature into a reforming tsar. He did not act like the ruler whose spectacular reign was to etch itself on history; on the contrary, it looked as if Russia was to be encumbered with a light-headed and indifferent sovereign.

During the seven years' rule of Sophia the country had made some progress. Vasily Golitsyn, her chancellor, had helped to narrow the gap that had for so long cut off Russia from the Western nations. He had made genuine efforts to liberate the serfs; permit freedom of worship; found a regular army; colonize the more remote provinces; and foster foreign trade. He had already done away with one social injustice: priority in the nominations of officials and officers based on family ties.

But it did not seem that Peter was going to offer any programs at all, progressive or not. He entrusted the affairs of state to his politically inexperienced mother and three prominent boyars, her brother Lev Naryshkin, Tikhon Streshnev, and Boris Golitsyn, a cousin of Sophia's chancellor. The Naryshkins now avenged themselves by persecuting the defeated Miloslavskys.

As for Peter, he forsook the pomp and ceremony of the Kremlin, preferring war games, boat building, and carousing in the foreign quarter. There he came into contact with two officers who were to exert great influence on him. One was a Scotsman, General Patrick Gordon—a devoted Roman Catholic. The other was a Swiss captain, Francis Lefort. Both were adventurers who hired themselves out as soldiers. It was Gordon, for many years a servant of Russia, who had helped persuade the foreign officers to support Peter when Sophia had challenged the youthful Tsar.

To the young monarch, Gordon epitomized the most commendable aspects of the Western way of life. The Scotsman had a profound knowledge of Europe and was skilled in the art of war. It was natural that Peter should accept him as his counselor, and they spent a good deal of time together.

Gordon was not only much older than Lefort—

twenty-one years—but was quite different in temperament. The Scotsman was serious-minded and modest. Lefort, in contrast, was noted for his gaiety, lively mind, and love of luxury. In his home he set out to impress the young Peter, introducing him to members of the cosmopolitan community. It was a different world with new ideas and ways of living. Unlike Russian women, the Western women had freedom and independence.

In these surroundings a girl was also to make Peter dissatisfied with his family and Russian customs, and to turn his eyes westward. Her name was Anna Mons.

It is known that she was the daughter of a Westphalian, but no one is quite certain who she was. Her father has been variously described as a wine merchant, goldsmith, and cooper (if papers preserved in his native town are correct). It has also been suggested that he kept a tavern, and that his two daughters waited on customers and drank with them. The elder daughter was the wife of a soldier of fortune, Captain Balck. Anna was a close friend of Lefort's and he had introduced her to the Tsar.

Although Peter's attachment for Anna Mons may seem unfitting behavior for a tsar, it must be remembered that his wife, Eudoxia, was not his choice. In a sense, the marriage was a tragic one. Eudoxia sincerely tried to give Peter affection and domestic happiness, yet she lacked the qualities which would endear herself to the Tsar. Although physically attractive, she was conventional and devoid of the high spirits which appealed to her husband. Furthermore, she was not overly intelligent.

Although the people disapproved of the Tsar's liaison with Anna Mons, it was Peter's mother—for no apparent reason jealous of Eudoxia—who contributed to the deterioration of his marriage. There were other contributing factors, too. Eudoxia was drawn to the Kremlin with its ancient traditions and court ritual, but Peter detested it. He preferred Preobrazhenskoye where for the time being he had settled. The marriage was further undermined by the Patriarch of the church, who used Eudoxia in efforts to lure the young Tsar away from his foreign friends.

Papers and documents of the time indicate that Anna Mons, a woman with little education, was cold and calculating as well as crude. At one point Peter intended to marry her. He showered her with gifts and permitted her to interfere in state affairs. When he met the nobility and foreign diplomats, she accompanied him.

During these formative years Peter declined morally, and with this decline came the violent temper and the cruelty for which he became well known. He made no attempt to rule. His interests were solely his warlike games and his drinking parties. Neither luxury nor lavish clothes had any appeal for him. Instead, he favored a Spartan existence, sometimes sharing a tent with a common soldier. Peter dreaded to sleep alone

B

because of his fear of fits—his stepbrothers and sisters had been subject to them.

With the virtual disappearance of normal court life in Moscow, some of the boyars and other dignitaries joined Peter's circle at Preobrazhenskoye. Whether they liked it or not, the Tsar compelled them to take part in the feasting and drinking.

An enormous drinker himself, Peter allowed no one to avoid his carousals. All sense of decency vanished in outbursts of brutality and debauchery. The court was the scene of degrading, drunken conversation and puerile behavior. Members of distinguished families painted their faces and wore garish dress: cat's paws and the tails of rats hung from their coats, and mice were sewn to their sleeves.

Indulging a childish love, Peter surrounded himself with freaks. As a boy he had been given a small carriage drawn by tiny ponies and accompanied by dwarfs. His enthusiasm for dwarfs had never waned. In the court he gathered many around him, along with fools and hunchbacks, and men with bizarre voices and faces.

In this clownish atmosphere mock titles were given out. One newcomer, Prince Feodor Romodanovsky, was christened the King of Pressburg; Pressburg was the fortress Peter had built some years earlier. Although the title was ludicrous, for years this "dignitary" sitting on a throne fulfilled ceremonial duties as a puppet sovereign. Another title was Prince-Pope, first bestowed on the drunken Matthew Naryshkin, a relative of Natalia's. Later it was given to Nikita Zotov, Peter's former tutor.

The high "dignitaries" wore tin miters crudely depicting a naked Bacchus astride a barrel. Vodka was the holy water. The hymns, prayers, and liturgies of the Orthodox Church were grossly parodied. Eventually these curious rites were extended to the point where they shocked not only the clergy but the people as well. Typical of these burlesques was the Palm Sunday procession in which the Prince-Pope traveled around Moscow on a camel.

Increasingly, to the end of his days the Tsar ridiculed the Orthodox Church. This was an odd attitude, one that has never really been explained, for Peter never doubted Christian teachings. It has been said that he lampooned the Church because the Patriarch symbolized the Russian traditions and ancient power which he loathed. Others claim that he was scoffing at the Pope, who was of no consequence to any Russian. However, it does seem strange that he would deliberately annoy and insult his Catholic friends in the foreign quarter.

No matter what Peter's reasons were, some Muscovites were scandalized at the sight of a tsar inspiring practices so outrageous that they implied insanity.

The six years beginning with 1690 were certainly a peculiar period in Peter's reign. Yet despite his drunkenness and apparent waywardness, he constantly sought news and new ideas from the West. Ships already intrigued him. Perhaps he had realized by now that his country could never be great until it had outlets to the Black Sea and the Baltic. If his ambitions extended to these regions, he must have known that they would never be taken without force.

Perhaps that was why he expanded his armies. He recruited riffraff as well as the sons of noble families. Romodanovsky, who was to become a ruthless yet highly efficient chief of police, was in command of the Preobrazhensky and Semenovsky battalions, which gradually increased to regiments. Maneuvers with some of the streltsy regiments were so realistic that many of the participants were killed or wounded.

Violence and noise satisfied the brutality that was a part of the Tsar. This was expressed in his experiments with explosives and in fireworks displays; sometimes these too caused deaths. His chemical tests demonstrated his enthusiasm for doing things himself. In 1691, working as a carpenter, he built his own yacht. The following year he looked for bigger vessels, and made his first long journey—to Archangel near the polar circle, Russia's only, and somewhat limited, outlet to the sea. He mixed freely with the English and Dutch skippers and merchants, and learned whatever he could about navigation. Among other things, he ordered a ship to be delivered from Holland to Archangel the following summer.

But before Peter could return to the north, his mother died. He was profoundly affected, and his facial convulsions returned. Nothing could console him.

When he finally did pay his second visit to Archangel, he was called "the skipper." Romodanovsky was "the admiral," and Gordon became "rear admiral of the fleet." A ship for which Peter had laid the keel the previous year—the *Saint Paul*—was launched with the exuberant Tsar on board. His excitement was even greater when the *Santa Profeetie,* the ship he had ordered, arrived from Holland. Here was a genuine warship, a frigate of forty-four guns. The Russian fleet had been born.

Peter returned home in August for the last of his mock battles. He was twenty-two. From this point on, the war would be real.

The next year Russia's ancient struggle with the Tatars was resumed. The Russians' main objective was an outlet on the Black Sea. But this waterway was surrounded by Turks and Tatars who dominated the north of the Crimea to the Sea of Azov, and across the Balkan Peninsula to Bosnia. The Christians in the region, oppressed by the Turks, called for Russian aid.

Although the campaign was to end disastrously, Peter revealed himself as an innovator by using the Russian waterways to transport his troops. The friction and lack of cooperation between his senior commanders contributed considerably to the defeat of the Russians. Peter, who had commanded artillery as a bombardier of the Preobrazhensky regiment, returned to Moscow without the glory he had expected to win.

After the defeat he recruited more experts from abroad: shipbuilders from Venice, and engineers, skilled in laying mines, from the Elector of Brandenburg. He had failed to take the town of Azov from the land; he would now attack from the sea. By embarking at Voronezh, he could use the Don River and save weeks of travel.

Thousands of Russians were mobilized to cut timber and work in the shipyards at Voronezh, where dreadful conditions caused large numbers to riot and desert. Although ill, Peter set an example for the rest, working among them with adz and plane. He did not even return to the capital when his stepbrother Ivan died in January. Living in a simple wooden house, the Tsar often rose before dawn to work by the light of pitch flares.

By spring, twenty-three galleys (one of them Dutch) and four flame-throwing ships were ready to unite with the great armada of transport vessels. This time Lefort was given complete charge. And this time the outcome was victory. Azov fell on July 17, 1696.

Peter now returned to his capital in triumph. The once maligned Tsar smiled at the cheering crowds. Typically, wearing the modest uniform of a post captain, he followed on foot behind the state sleigh carrying the hero Lefort.

Peter's achievement, however, was out of all proportion to its impact on Christendom. Statesmen of the West received the news with surprise and apprehension. Russia might now rise as a serious military threat.

The Azov conquest had not gained access to the Black Sea. Turkish fortifications still dominated the

Straits of Kerch, which separated the Sea of Azov from the Black Sea. Peter continued to build ships. He forced rich landowners, merchants, and the clergy to finance his program. At the end of two years, he owned fifty-two warships, but he needed qualified officers to man them. He dispatched fifty men of noble birth to study abroad. This move, coming as a surprise to the families of the men, evoked their hostility and resentment. The women, distressed by the separation from their men, dressed themselves in mourning. But Peter was adamant. It is quite possible that he derived sadistic pleasure from it all. At times he was undoubtedly cruel, but it must be stressed that, in those days, cruelty was part of the national scene, not only in Russia but elsewhere. To subject men and women to agony, to cut out tongues, and burn people at the stake were common practices. In Russia, they were employed by whatever faction was in power. There was no public outcry against torture, but many thought it shameful that it was applied by a tsar. Peter not only attended Romodanovsky's torture chambers at Preobrazhenskoye but he took a hand himself, wielding the knout and cudgel with great enthusiasm.

3

TRAVELS IN EUROPE

It is true that Tsar Peter could be a cruel and seemingly heartless man. But in fairness, it must be remembered that there were many who conspired against him. Cruelty was a means of survival, and an efficient method of extracting evidence. In the winter months, after the Tsar's return from Azov, frictions and antagonisms grew rife. The Naryshkins were guilty of bribery and corruption. There was hostility toward aliens. Also, to many people, Peter's eccentricities were not in keeping with the dignity of the throne.

Peter was, to say the least, an unusual sovereign. He would often be seen in the role of the laborer, wearing workman's clothes and heavy boots. He was coarse and rough, and, by most standards, barbaric.

Even so, untutored and unkempt as he was, Peter had great vision and a genuine desire to move his country forward. He wished to travel in Europe to promote diplomatic ties and win aid for his war against the Tatars. His trip was delayed by unrest and intrigue, by conspiracies against him. To put an end to the delay, Peter dealt with the conspirators swiftly and fiercely. As Romodanovsky hunted them down, the punishments were perhaps a warning to others who might harbor thoughts of plotting against him while he was away. Chief among the traitors was Tsykler, the streltsy colonel who had forsaken Sophia and joined the Tsar. Unpopular with Peter, he had gone unrewarded. He was ordered to Taganrog on the Sea of Azov, to help in constructing the new port. The Tsar's order was akin to banishment; instead of going, Tsykler plotted to assassinate Peter.

But the streltsy commander was caught in Romodanovsky's net. Under torture he revealed his associates: Feodor Pushkin (an ancestor of the great Russian poet) and Alexis Sokovnin. The grievances of these two men sprang from the Tsar's order that their children be sent to foreign countries for teaching. Under torture Tsykler also implicated three others, two from the streltsy regiment. Peter learned that seven years earlier Sophia and Tsykler had discussed the murder of the Tsar, and that Ivan Miloslavsky had proposed a plan to accomplish that objective.

In one of the furious, hysterical outbursts that characterized him, Peter had the body of Ivan Miloslavsky exhumed, then dragged by pigs into Red Square. The enraged Tsar also came close to having Sophia tortured.

Perhaps aiming to terrify his enemies into submission, he made a lavish display of the executions. A lofty stone pillar with six iron pegs had been erected in Red Square. Onlookers witnessed a gruesome spectacle as the limbs were severed from Tsykler and the other five condemned men. Still alive, they were lifted to a scaffold and then decapitated, their blood dripping onto the corpse of Ivan Miloslavsky stretched in a box below. Their heads, hanging on the metal pegs, stayed there as a warning to others.

Some days later, the Tsar and his Great Embassy began their long journey through Europe. Peter, who traveled incognito as a private individual, was curious to know why certain countries—tiny compared with his vast empire—were so rich and powerful.

The Embassy comprised well over one hundred and fifty members. With the ambassadors were twenty-four gentlemen, a dozen officials, priests, goldsmiths, and interpreters. A merchant was entrusted with the care and sale of a huge quantity of sable skins which, with bags of gold and silver, were to cover expenses. The rest of the party was made up of apprentices, retainers, and guards in charge of the wagons. To Western eyes it was an exotic cavalcade. However, the Tsar traveled modestly as a carpenter, calling himself Peter Mikhailof.

For political reasons the Embassy did not pass

through Poland. The Polish sovereign had died, and a controversy raged over his successor. Among those nominated for the throne were Prince de Conti, who was supported by the French, and Augustus, Elector of Saxony, the candidate of the Russians. The French were friends of the Turks, and Peter had made it known that de Conti's election would destroy peace between Russia and Poland.

The Embassy journeyed north, through territory under the rule of Sweden. At Libau Peter had his first glimpse of the Baltic. Ordering the Embassy to continue by land, the Tsar—a sailor at heart—went to Königsberg by sea. There he met the Elector of Brandenburg, who hoped for an alliance with Russia for mutual defense.

If accounts by contemporary writers are to be believed, Peter greatly taxed the patience of the people of Brandenburg. It is said that, as host to local dignitaries, he refused to let any guest leave before the visitor had consumed a huge quantity of wine. When the Brandenburg chancellor tried to leave, the irate Tsar is alleged to have pushed him out of the room.

Wearing animal skins and holding a vast saber, the points of his moustache turned up toward his ears, Peter is said to have presented himself at the Brandenburg court looking like a bear. In drunken moments he is also reported to have been noisy and violent among guests. Presumably, in one such incident, Lefort felt the point of Peter's sword.

No doubt Peter was often offensive. His humor was

crude and apt to be in poor taste. He was also blasphemous, as well as irritable by nature. But perhaps the accounts of his behavior on the European tour were exaggerations. Other accounts describe him as gauche and crude, but never violent. Charlotte of Prussia, stepdaughter of the Elector of Hanover, gives an impression of Peter as an awkward young man, nervous and ill at ease due to the sudden impact of Western ways. The uncontrollable shaking of his head and his frightful facial expressions probably gave misleading impressions.

By Western standards, Peter lacked polish, but behind the uncouthness there were exceptional talents and signs of the statesman. While at Königsberg he communicated with Romodanovsky, in whom he had entrusted power in his absence. Along with the letters Romodanovsky also sent messages in invisible ink. Thus, Peter was able to receive secret information about home matters.

Peter ordered Romodanovsky to send troops to the Polish frontier if de Conti were elected. The seal on his letters typified the young Tsar: it was the figure of an artisan—himself—with tools, and the words, "Myself a pupil; I seek the teachers."

When Peter heard that Augustus, the Russian choice, had been placed on the Polish throne, he left Königsberg and journeyed across northern Germany to Hanover. Sailing by river and canal, he arrived in Holland. Peter could speak Dutch, having learned the language from a Latin scholar whose father was a Dutch merchant living in Moscow.

Peter had profound respect for the Dutch and their way of life, so he was enthusiastic when he arrived in Zaandam. Using the name of Peter Baas, the Tsar, a man who ruled an empire, labored as an ordinary workman in a shipyard and lived like one. For a week he lodged with Gerrit Kist, an old friend and a former ironsmith in the Russian capital.

When the news leaked out that Peter Baas was, in fact, the Tsar, Peter left for Amsterdam, where he remained for four months. The greater part of his time was devoted to shipbuilding in the docks of the East India Company. The work, however, did not give him the knowledge he sought. He wished to design ships, yet he soon realized that the Dutch did not create, but only copied models. England, he discovered, was the place where ships were built according to mathematical theory.

Peter also devoted time to astronomy because it was valuable in navigation. And since he entertained the fantastic idea of linking the Caspian and Black seas, he studied the engineering aspects of canals.

Workshops, hospitals, and schools attracted him. At a school of anatomy, Peter was shown how to cut up a corpse. Although he was intrigued, most of his fellow Russians were repelled. It reflected Peter's grotesque humor when he compelled his comrades to bite through the muscles of several bodies. Such things amused him.

So did the extraction of a tooth with the tip of a sword, a crude technique he had acquired from a dentist.

In those four months in Amsterdam Peter lived again as ordinary folk lived. His homes were humble dwellings where, rising at daybreak, he lit the fire each day. His passion for work in the shipyards had a specific motive. Under his guidance Russia would one day possess a powerful fleet. With it he believed he would be the champion of Christendom, and that he would conquer the Turks in the Black Sea, seize Constantinople, and liberate the Christians.

In Holland, Peter met William of Orange, the King of England. William invited the Tsar to London where Peter continued his apprenticeship in the shipyards of Deptford and Woolwich Arsenal. He later admitted, "If I had not come here, I should always have remained a plain carpenter."

Unlike the leading members of his party, Peter still dressed plainly and denied himself luxury. This was characteristic. By all accounts his appearance was shabby. He would willingly spend money on things that were useful but at other times he could be very tight-fisted with his money; it was a trait that irritated London society.

This close watch on the purse, however, did not apply to the Embassy. The trip was no cheap undertaking, having cost 2½ million rubles (equivalent to 2¼ million dollars today). Peter considered that the aims justified the expense. To help reduce his costs, however, he sold the license to import tobacco into

Russia for 20,000 pounds sterling. He added an additional 500 guineas to his coffers by matching one of his soldiers against an Englishman in a prizefight. The tobacco deal provoked comment, for the Orthodox Church had long refused to allow smoking in Russia. Whose order was to be followed—the Patriarch's or the Tsar's? Peter left no one in doubt. With his usual forthrightness, he made it apparent that smoking was no concern of the Church. He smoked; so could the people if they desired.

In religious matters, although Peter was a firm believer, he did not necessarily accept the dictates of the Church, for in his view the Church was much too reactionary. Also, many priests were hypocritical, calling upon the people to obey the laws of the Church, yet ignoring them themselves.

On the death of the aged Patriarch Joachim, in March, 1690, Peter had intended to choose a successor who was not only a scholar but who was prepared to tolerate other creeds. The Tsar would have had his way but for the strong opposition of his mother. The appointment had gone to his mother's choice, Adrian of Kazan, who was also a reactionary.

It has been suggested that temperamentally the Tsar was a Protestant. It is true that at Deptford he mingled with the Quakers and impressed William Penn, their leader. The simple, yet profound, religion, stripped of ritual, appealed to Peter. The Tsar's "extraordinary zeal for piety and purity," said Penn, did not lessen his love for carousing. During his shipbuilding days at Deptford, Peter and his companions lived at Sayes Court near the King's Yard. This was the home of John Evelyn, the diarist, who had rented it to Admiral Benbow. The latter, in turn, had sublet it to the Tsar.

The house was the scene of much wildness. Apparently, one of Peter's pastimes was to be pushed in a wheelbarrow through a holly hedge. The house and grounds were seriously damaged. Furniture was smashed and pictures destroyed. Windows and grates were broken; the kitchen floor was blown up; and sheets and featherbeds were ripped to pieces. The record also indicates that the Russians stole Benbow's charts and designs.

From Deptford Peter went to Vienna. So far he had not concluded a military alliance against the Turks. He hoped to accomplish this in Vienna. On his arrival, he was at first treated as the carpenter Peter Mikhailof, the incognito he had assumed for traveling. The Austrians maintained the pretense. When Lefort and other Russian leaders were invited to a banquet by the Emperor Leopold, Peter found himself in the ridiculous position of standing behind Lefort's chair.

Despite the cordiality and the festivities, when the monarchs actually met, Peter realized that his treaty would not be forthcoming. Leopold was more anxious to arrange a peace settlement with the Turks. Like the English and the Dutch, Austria was alert to the approaching War of the Spanish Succession.

4

FIRST SIGNS OF REFORM

Peter had failed in the diplomatic sphere, but in other respects the Embassy was a success. Some of its members stayed in Prussia, Holland, and England to learn to be shipbuilders and technicians. In turn, many Western experts—doctors, engineers, naval men, and others—went to Russia to help introduce new and modern ways. In England the Embassy had learned much about government. William of Orange sent instruments, books, and other specimens of European civilization to Archangel on the *Royal Transport,* his new yacht.

From Vienna, Peter had intended to travel to Venice, but he suddenly canceled the visit. News had reached him of a streltsy uprising and a plot to return Sophia

c

to power. Discontent had risen among the streltsy because they no longer served in the capital where their families lived. They had been sent away from Moscow because Peter did not trust them. Now that the Tsar was out of the country they had marched on Moscow, but Gordon's forces had routed them.

Peter hurried home, this time through Poland, where he met Augustus. This meeting was to have great impact on Europe.

Back in Russia after an absence of eighteen months, the Tsar lost no time avenging himself. He decided that Romodanovsky had not punished the streltsy sufficiently for the uprising. The insurgents, numbering in the hundreds, were now tortured and executed. The fourteen torture chambers at Preobrazhenskoye, where Peter stayed for hours on end, were loud with agonized screams as victims were roasted over slow fires until they confessed. Holding candles, the victims were borne in carts, followed by their weeping families, into Moscow. More than three hundred were hanged.

Peter, on horseback, and in a tunic of green, watched the gruesome proceedings. As the weeks went by, hundreds more were hanged, some even outside the window of Sophia's cell.

During this dreadful period there were times when Peter seemed to be insane. His face would show the frightful convulsions, and there were moments of ungovernable rage. Once, during a feast, he slashed out crazily with his sword. Some chroniclers say that he was restrained by Lefort; others say Menshikov, another intimate, checked him. Both men, however, and anyone else who happened to be near Peter, sustained blows from the fist or cudgel.

There is no doubt that Sophia was involved in the uprising. One would have expected Peter to punish her harshly, but he did not; instead, he took away her rank and compelled her to become Sister Susanne. The women who had been the intermediaries between Sophia and the streltsy were not as fortunate; for their part in the plot, they were buried alive. The streltsy ceased to exist; all the regiments were disbanded. No one, neither officers nor men, was permitted to re-enlist elsewhere, and wives and children of the executed were forced to leave their homes.

Peter also compelled another person to take the veil—his wife. During his travels he had not communicated at all with Eudoxia. Neither had he greeted her on his return to Russia. Peter had resolved that the marriage must end. Eudoxia was taken to a convent in the town of Suzdal, and Alexis, now eight years old, was put under the care of Princess Natalia, Peter's sister.

By now Peter was very unpopular with his subjects; many, in fact, hated him. Mingled with their enmity was their fear of him. Perhaps he despised the traditions of his country even more now that he had experienced life in Western Europe. He would allow no interference with his plans for national reform, not even from the Church.

Immediately upon his return to Moscow, Peter had

perpetrated another affront to the priests and to Old Russia. The Church had always decreed that men should wear beards, commoners as well as the nobility. But the distinguished boyars who had greeted the Tsar had departed minus their beards. Peter cut them off. Only two aged dignitaries were untouched.

Those who attended a banquet some days later were forced to have their beards cut off by a court fool. Actually, many of the nobles were happy to go beardless, and only the condemnation of the Church had deterred them from shaving before. But this was not true of the ordinary people. They copied the saints, who were always portrayed on the ikons with beards. The longer the beards the happier the people felt. Agreeing with the dictate of the Church, they believed that the shaving of beards, the custom in the West, was nothing short of heresy. Even after they had been ordered to shave, many peasants and workmen hid their beards under their tunics.

Despite the powerful opposition of the priests, Peter made the wearing of beards illegal, and a tax was imposed on all who retained them: a hundred rubles for a noble, a kopeck for a peasant. As proof of payment a disc was usually attached to the beard.

Next, Peter attacked the Russian style of dress. The medieval caftans and tunics, although colorful, were scoffed at abroad. Moreover, the Tsar claimed that the wide sleeves were inconvenient and caused numerous accidents. At a ceremony in February, 1699,

Peter displayed his dislike of Russian dress by cutting off the huge sleeves of his attendants. The masses were in no rush to follow the court's example, but the well-to-do did discard the traditional garb in favor of German costume.

Obviously emulating the courts of Europe, Peter originated his country's first order of chivalry, the Order of St. Andrew, named for the patron saint of Russia. Another of his innovations was the abolition of the ancient calendar. This reform took Russia another step away from the medieval period and into the modern world. Before the reform, it had long been the Russian practice to count the years from what was regarded as the creation of the world. Peter decreed that as of January, 1700 (the year 7208 according to the old calendar), Russia—like all the countries of Europe—would count the years from the birth of Christ.

The old order was changing, and there were signs of reform. In Red Square, the eighteenth century was ushered in with a religious service and with salvos of artillery and musketry. Fireworks lit up the night sky. Russia was awakening from her medieval dream, and Peter was the cause of it. To a wealthy merchant in Amsterdam he had granted a monopoly to export to Russia books printed in the Russian language. *The Life of Alexander the Great* by Quintus Curtius, as well as dictionaries and works on astronomy, arithmetic, and history, were being translated into Russian. Some of the foreign experts engaged by Peter had already arrived. Among them were three English mathematicians who were also skilled in the science of navigation.

The seeds of change had been sown, but there would be years of sacrifice before the plants would begin to thrive.

In the midst of this changing world, Peter still held to his old plan to drive out the Turks. He went again to Voronezh to supervise the building of a fleet. While there, he received news of Lefort's death. During a drinking bout at a banquet, Lefort had gone outside into the freezing air and caught a chill. Peter was filled with grief and personally arranged the funeral ceremony. Some months later, Gordon also died, and the Tsar wept by the bedside of his friend.

Lefort had impressed upon the Tsar the value of the Great Embassy, but Lefort had not been successful in diplomacy. On January 14, 1699, the countries that Peter had hoped would become his allies reached peace terms with the Turks.

In the spring, Peter's new fleet set sail against the Turks, but fighting was never necessary. When a new Russian frigate anchored at Constantinople, the Turks sued for peace. Russia secured the long-sought access to the Black Sea. Azov and other ports were signed over to her, and she no longer had to pay tribute to the Crimea.

While Peter waited for the peace treaty with the Turks to be signed, his eyes turned northward—to the Baltic. The outcome was to be more than two decades of war. In that period Russia would undergo reforms dictated by the necessities of war. Thus, in the first quarter of the eighteenth century, out of misery and strife, and after centuries of stagnation, a new Russia emerged.

5

A VITAL LESSON

Peter's long campaign against Sweden—the Northern War—was a daring enterprise, for Sweden was powerful and virtually the master of northern Europe. But the Tsar felt that he had no choice. If Russia was to thrive economically, his country had to have a gateway on the northern coast.

This new political ambition is generally believed to have been discussed when the Tsar met with Augustus in Poland. The Polish king wished to regain Livonia from Swedish rule, and Peter had designs on recovering other once-Russian territories. These ambitions were fanned in the Polish court by Johann Reinhold von Patkul, who represented the rebellious Livonian landowners.

Accused of high treason, he was under sentence of death from the Swedes. Joining the Russian-Polish alliance was Denmark, deprived by Sweden of the Duchy of Holstein.

Patkul went to see Peter in November, 1699, on a visit that was kept secret from the Swedish representative in Moscow. Without consulting his ministers, Peter entered into the coalition with Poland and Denmark, assuring both countries of his complete support once he had concluded peace with the Turks. He did not wish to risk fighting on two fronts. At the same time, he promised visiting Swedish delegates that he would confirm the treaties that existed between their two countries.

During this period Peter continued his domestic reforms. He had been impressed by the English currency system, and so he introduced a new coinage in March, then founded a mint.

Months passed and still the peace treaty with Turkey had not been signed. Peter refused to march but kept increasing his stock of weapons. By August 8, 1700 when the Turks finally accepted the thirty-year armistice, the Russian forces were well armed. The following day Peter ordered them to cross the Swedish frontier and besiege the fortress of Narva, located to the southwest of present-day Leningrad.

In this lengthy Northern War, two great military figures were to dominate the scene: Peter and young King Charles XII of Sweden. Both monarchs had dismayed their people by their curious behavior. Charles would ride naked in the streets of Stockholm, and in his palace a favorite pastime was hacking down calves and sheep. Equally eccentric was his delight in hunting hares in the Chamber of the Diet.

To the Swedish people, the king's antics verged on lunacy, yet they were dumbfounded by the change in him when he was confronted by war. He became one of Sweden's greatest military heroes. War occupied most of his life, and for years he seemed to be invincible.

Eighteen years old at the start of the Northern War, Charles quickly compelled Denmark to surrender. Augustus, who had opened hostilities before Peter, was brilliantly checked, opening the way for a direct confrontation between the Swedes and the Russians.

At the Battle of Narva, Charles, with eight thousand men, routed a Russian army of at least four times that size. Peter had already left the front, placing in command the Duc von Croy, a German mercenary. The battle took place in a blizzard, and when Peter's confused peasant soldiers saw Swedish faces, they thought that their own mercenaries had united with the enemy. They began to slaughter their foreign officers.

The Russian cavalry tried to swim the Narva River, but hundreds were drowned. The rout was complete. Only two of Peter's regiments—the Preobrazhensky and the Semenovsky—had distinguished themselves.

Peter had suffered an ignominious defeat, and he was accused of cowardice for having left his army to the mercy of the Swedes. He became the subject of ridicule in the capitals of Europe. The humiliation was all the greater because Peter had provoked the war after having confirmed all treaties with Sweden.

The Tsar, however, treated failure as a lesson for the future. In previous campaigns Russia had relied considerably on foreign troops. Peter was determined to change that: Russia must have her own national army. For the Narva campaign, the training of the peasant force had been entrusted chiefly to German and Scottish sergeants. But this was an almost impossible task in the relatively short time allowed them. The peasants, moreover, were so ignorant, that to learn left from right, straw was fastened to one leg and hay to the other.

Failure inspired Peter to greater effort. He wrote to Boris Sheremetev, who had commanded the cavalry, "We must not lose our heads in misfortune. I order the work we have undertaken to go on. We do not lack men. The rivers and marshes are frozen; I will hear no excuses."

Fortunately, the season favored the Russians. It was autumn and the Swedes wisely avoided invading Russia at that time of the year. Instead, they hurried southward to attack the Poles. This gave Peter the chance to fortify his frontier and rebuild his forces. Training was intensified. Huge supplies of arms and equipment were ordered from Western Europe, including fifteen thousand rifles, cannon, field glasses, and, from Liège in Belgium, ostrich feathers for the officers' hats.

To overcome the shortage of metal in Russia, bells were taken from belfries, melted down, and cast into cannon. In one year, three hundred guns, together with a thousand shot for each, were made available.

Peter realized that money is the sinews of war, and to finance his preparations, he extracted more and more revenue from his already heavily taxed people and confiscated property from the monasteries. This act coincided with some undermining of the Church's power.

In October, on the eve of the Battle of Narva, the Patriarch Adrian died. He had been severely criticized for failing to safeguard ancient traditions, such as the wearing of beards, but it must be stressed that he had been sick throughout this period. Peter realized that a strong patriarch could still create some embarrassment and even obstruct reform. So the Tsar decided to appoint no successor for the time being. Instead, he designated Stephen Yavorsky, a Ukrainian scholar and abbot, as Exarch, and assigned him the task of liquidating the Patriarchate. The Tsar had promoted him because of his Western outlook.

Stephen's main tasks were to control the administration of Church affairs and to deal with heretics. He introduced a number of reforms. He ordered a census of monks and nuns and all residents and dependents of the monasteries. Those who made no tangible contributions to the monasteries were forced to leave, and the monks were compelled to be more industrious than formerly. Under Stephen's guidance, new schools and colleges were founded. Church income helped finance Peter's wars, and the sons of priests were given permission to join the army.

In December, 1701, the new commander in chief of the army, Sheremetev, moved his forces to the Livonian frontier to attack the Swedes. The Russians were victorious. In recognition of the victory, Peter promoted Sheremetev to general field marshal and presented him with a diamond-studded portrait of the Tsar himself.

Returning to Moscow, the Tsar arranged a great feast in Red Square. The defeat at Narva had been avenged. He was now aware that a second assault on Narva was not essential; it would be better to go around it, concentrating on Ingria and the Neva basin (north of present-day Leningrad). In Livonia, the farms and everything else that had been of use to the Swedes were deliberately destroyed. The people, herded like cattle, were forced to make the long trek deep into Russia.

One of the Livonian captives was a seventeen-year-old servant girl named Martha. An orphan, she had lived in the household of a Pastor Glück. No one is certain of Martha's origin. It is possible that her parents were Lithuanian peasants who went to live in Livonia. Her family name also remains uncertain. This obscure peasant girl was to become famous in history as Catherine I, empress of all Russia. Catherine was the name she took after being admitted to the Orthodox Church. She was to be Peter's consort and, after his death, the ruler of Russia.

On leaving Livonia, Peter secretly prepared a northern base at Lake Ladoga. Leading his troops in the autumn of 1702, he captured the fortress of Noteburg and renamed it Schlüsselburg.

The Russians overran the forests and the swamps and came to the small town of Nyenskantz, an island fortress at the mouth of the Neva. Peter transported his troops in some sixty boats. On May 1, 1703, the Swedes surrendered, but a few days later Swedish warships arrived in the delta. The Tsar and Menshikov embarked during darkness with detachments of the Preobrazhensky and Semenovsky regiments in a surprise attack. The two main Swedish vessels were boarded and captured. Two lesser ships, though sustaining serious damage, managed to get away.

The Russians had won the first naval victory in their country's history. Peter had smashed his way to the sea. As he put it, he had opened "a window on Europe."

6

THE CURTAIN IS LIFTED

Except for two Swedish fortresses and a few humble homes of Finnish fishermen, there were no settlements in the Neva delta, a region of forests and swamps. Yet two weeks after the fall of Nyenskantz, the Tsar's new town of Piterburkh (Petersburg), the future capital, was founded on the banks and islands of the Neva River delta. It is said that the location was suggested by Grand Admiral Golovin, who wished to have an arsenal there.

On May 16, the Feast of the Trinity, work was begun on wooden huts and earthworks. Peter, taking a soldier's bayonet, cut two sods, placed them crosswise, and remarked: "Here I will build the town."

At this entrance to the Gulf of Finland, Peter began to build frigates. Protected by shore batteries, the work proceeded throughout the summer although a Swedish fleet waited outside the estuary.

In 1704, the Russians recaptured Dorpat and Narva. At Narva, to his shame, the Tsar was guilty of shocking behavior. Probably recalling his humiliating defeat, he slaughtered women and children, and is said to have struck the commandant and publicly ducked his wife in the river.

To celebrate the victory at Dorpat and Narva, Peter returned to Moscow with Catherine, who had now replaced Anna Mons as his constant companion. There was the customary feasting and fireworks. Prince Romodanovsky, still posing as His Majesty, "promoted" Peter to the rank of captain for bravery.

It is said that Peter, having taken the Neva delta and the surrounding region, would have agreed to a peace settlement. But Charles XII had no intention of ending hostilities: he now concentrated on defeating Augustus of Saxony and capturing Poland. Once he had accomplished this he planned to direct all his energies toward conquering Russia.

Peter sent troops to Augustus, enabling the Poles to recapture Warsaw. But Charles could not be stopped and Augustus signed a peace treaty with him at Altrandstädt on September 24, 1706. Augustus was forced to abdicate the Polish throne, and to deliver Patkul, who was promptly killed.

Charles's success was a great political gain. The Western nations sent their representatives to Altrandstädt, hoping to secure Swedish neutrality in the War of the Spanish Succession. Had Charles chosen to march westward at that time, he might well have been able to take vast territories. Instead, during the latter part of 1707, he turned toward Russia, which he planned to disarm and partition.

European statesmen believed that Russia was incapable of withstanding Swedish might. Peter had no idea when or where the enemy would strike, and as each day passed, the strain increased. Under terrible conditions, hordes of workmen toiled throughout the harsh winter on fortifications at Kiev and Smolensk. Many of the ill-housed, ill-fed workmen died. To hinder a Swedish advance on Moscow, regions were laid waste along the routes to Pskov and Smolensk.

Russia did have a veteran army, and more recruits joined each day. When the clash came Charles would not encounter disorderly rabble as he had at Narva. This time arms of high quality were plentiful, and the army had been equipped with a new invention—the bayonet. Always willing to accept new ideas, Peter had introduced mounted cavalry. He had also sent men into Siberia in search of war materials, and they had located a great range of minerals.

Nevertheless, the Tsar was prepared to discuss peace. He was even willing to give back the Baltic territories provided that he kept Petersburg. But Charles stub-

D

bornly wanted the return of all territory, as well as compensation for all those whose property had been ruined.

In June, 1708, Charles put his plan into action. He intended to unite his forces at Mohilev with an army commanded by General Lowenhaupt. Another Swedish unit waited in Finland. However, Lowenhaupt was defeated near Lesnoy on the White Sea, thus depriving Charles of valuable artillery and supplies. Now the Swedish king made a serious mistake. Instead of hurrying after the Russians, he delayed for four months.

His intention was to avoid Moscow for the moment and proceed to the Ukraine. Expecting help from the neighboring Turks and from Ivan Mazepa, a Cossack leader who had already betrayed Peter, Charles held up action. The delay was costly. The bitter winter that followed undermined Swedish morale. On Peter's orders the peasants slaughtered cattle, destroyed supplies, and left the enemy short of food. Many Swedes perished, but Charles refused to listen to his officers and go back to Poland.

For some time Peter had been experiencing recurring bouts of illness, and there were moments when he believed he was about to die. In April, 1709, aware that his illness was returning, he traveled south to Azov for treatment. His recovery was slow. During his absence the Swedes pushed on to the outskirts of Poltava.

Menshikov, constantly harassing the enemy, realized

that the decisive battle would soon be joined. He sent a message to Peter asking him to hurry to the front. But the Tsar was not strong enough to leave Azov until May 27. He arrived at Poltava on June 4. Menshikov wanted a full-scale battle to begin at once, but the Tsar advised caution. This was one of Peter's outstanding traits. He was not only wary, but also calculating. Even at times of heavy drinking he retained a cool, scheming mind.

Peter did not begin the battle until the defenders of Poltava signaled for help. Charles had the misfortune to be wounded even before the main action began. The night before, he had fought Cossacks in the forest and had been shot in the foot.

On June 27, 1709, years of warfare culminated in the decisive struggle. The Russians were stronger in artillery and were inspired by the words of the Tsar: "The hour has come in which the destinies of our country will be decided. It is of her that you must think, it is for her that you must fight . . . and as for Peter, know that he does not cling to his own life, provided Russia lives in her glory and in prosperity."

That June day was one of frightful slaughter, especially of Swedish soldiers, who suffered more than nine thousand dead. Charles, who had been carried into battle on a litter, escaped to Turkey.

At the command of the Tsar the Russians gathered on the battlefield for a religious ceremony and to thank God for victory. Dining in his tent with captured Swedish officers, Peter drank to their health. They were, he said, his teachers in the art of war.

Victory celebrations were held in Moscow some months later. A foreign observer described them: "The triumphal procession was certainly the most imposing and magnificent ever since the days of the ancient Romans." The next day at mass, Peter, wearing a wig borrowed from a court servant, stood unrecognized among the great crowd in the cathedral. The guests at the victory banquet—among them representatives of all the European powers—were so numerous that the master of ceremonies moved around them on horseback. That night a gargantuan fireworks display illumined the sky.

Peter reinstated Augustus as the Polish sovereign. The alliance with Denmark was renewed, and by the end of 1710, all of Karelia and Livonia, in the extreme northwest, had been conquered. Peter had achieved his objectives. However, the peace he expected was not to be. The sultan of Turkey had given refuge to Charles. When Peter demanded that the Swedish king be turned over to him, the sultan refused, and Charles persuaded Turkey to declare war on Russia.

In the ensuing campaign, Peter seemed to lose his natural caution. During July, 1711, the Turkish army crossed the River Prut into Russian territory. The Russians, seriously short of provisions, were not only surrounded but were outnumbered five to one. Peter was trapped. According to tradition, it was a woman—Catherine—who thought of the way out; she induced him to buy peace. (However, many modern authorities doubt the truth of this story.)

He offered the Turkish leader a great sum of money and agreed to evacuate the ports and fortifications beside the Sea of Azov. He agreed to leave the territories, except for Ingris and Petersburg, that had been won from Sweden, and he guaranteed Charles safe conduct to his homeland. The sultan agreed to the terms, for despite his military advantage, he had sustained heavy losses.

Charles was furious when he learned that Peter and his army had escaped. He refused to let Russia keep Petersburg, and the Northern War continued. Peter was compelled to carry the fight into Swedish Pomerania and into German territory.

He and his country were now a force to be reckoned with in Europe, a fact which roused fears in certain countries. Austria was unhappy because the Russians were entrenched in Livonia, and England resented Russia's growth as a maritime power in the Baltic.

Therefore, Peter could not expect help from these countries in his search for peace. Ironically, he now approached France, a nation which for years had been antagonistic toward him. Louis XIV was dead, and the new French regent saw the political value in creating friendship between France and a powerful Russia.

On April 21, 1717, Peter arrived at Dunkirk. It was a profitable journey. After the sudden death of Charles XII, French diplomacy brought peace between Sweden and Russia. The peace treaty was signed at Nystad in

Finland on August 30, 1721. The Russian prizes were Estonia, Ingria, Livonia, Karelia, and an area that included the fortress of Viborg.

The firing of cannon on September 4 announced the Tsar's return to Petersburg. He prepared for a religious thanksgiving, drinking and feasting, processions, and fireworks.

In a military sense Peter's supreme task was accomplished. Now he could write, "We have lifted the curtain drawn in front of our country's curiosity, which deprived her of communication with the whole world."

7

MOLDING A NEW RUSSIA

During those seemingly interminable war years, there were significant internal changes in Russia. One of the foremost was the gradual decline in the power of the Duma, or Tsar's Council. The Duma of the boyars had for centuries controlled the legislative, administrative, and judicial life of Russia. The boyars came from the relatively few, highly privileged families who, in general, opposed any kind of change. It is not surprising, therefore, that Peter despised them. He issued decrees without consulting the Duma. Unlike previous sovereigns, he took no Duma members with him on his journeys or military campaigns.

When all its power had waned, Peter had finally

given the Duma the deathblow in 1711, before he departed for the war with Turkey. He formed a Senate of nine members, empowering it to govern in his absence. Only three Senate members were drawn from the ancient Duma; the rest were from the new governing class that Peter had founded.

Peter's original intention was that the Senate would deal with the affairs of government only during his absences from Moscow. Since he was frequently absent, the members spent much time in office. In time they were assigned additional duties, of an executive and judicial nature, supervised by a procurator-general.

Gone were the days when men rose to power through family influence. Now distinction was achieved not on hereditary grounds but on personal merit. The gap between the boyars and the rest of the aristocracy was closed for good. From that point on, political, social, and other forms of advancement were to be earned by a genuine "nobility of service."

There was ample evidence to prove that low birth and foreign nationality were no longer barriers to merited honors. The resourceful Menshikov, the onetime pieman who became a prince, was one example. But there were many others. Count Devier, a Portuguese Jew and former cabin boy whom Peter had met in Holland, became powerful in Petersburg as the first commissioner of police. Yaguzhinsky, whose father was the organist at the Lutheran Church in Moscow, was elevated to the post of procurator-general for the Senate. Ostermann, formerly a manservant, signed the

Treaty of Nystad for Russia and became a key figure in his country's diplomatic discussions. The serf Kurbatov filled an important post in the treasury.

By removing class distinctions Peter enabled the minor nobility, previously obstructed by the great families, to move up to positions of power. Many of them were volunteers in his Preobrazhensky and Semenovsky regiments. They formed the hard core of his supporters. And they were also to be the mainstay behind his successors.

Peter tried to make certain that all members of the aristocracy served the country in some way. This was not a new idea, but he strove to prevent them from evading their duty. All young nobles entered service at the age of fifteen. A third of them went into civil administration; the remainder, no matter how illustrious their births, served as common soldiers, mainly in the Guard. No longer did they automatically receive officer rank. A decree forbade their promotion to commissioned status until they had trained as ordinary soldiers. Anyone who rose to officer class immediately acquired a title, but no one below the rank of commandant was granted a hereditary title.

Peter began to remold the entire medieval administration of Russia. Having been impressed during the Great Embassy by English methods of administration, he asked an Englishman, Francis Lee, to prepare a plan that would give Russia modern government machinery.

Many of the laws that would reshape the domestic

pattern were actually written by Peter. Among them were the military regulations, much of the maritime regulations, and reforms of central and local administrations. Peter's weakness, however, lay in the fact that he did not have a general concept of Russian administration as a whole. Instead, he tended to select laws from the West, then adapt them for Russia.

Until Peter modernized it, the government had no ministries in the modern sense. What did exist were the *prikaz* (departments) which dealt with civil and military administration and foreign affairs. There was even a prikaz of the apothecaries, which controlled the relatively few pharmacies in the country. As a rule, each prikaz was headed by a member of the Duma. Actually these men held their offices in name only, leaving the practical work to numerous clerks whose main objective was to enrich themselves. Extortion and other forms of corruption were common. To defend themselves against these administrators many people turned to fraud and violence. Some formed themselves into pillaging bands which obstructed the collection of taxes.

Forty-four prikaz were in existence at the beginning of Peter's reign. Eventually their number was reduced to nine, and, in 1718, the Tsar started to replace these with colleges, which were similar in structure to the ministries of today. More colleges were added, and eventually their authority prevailed throughout Russia. The presidents of the colleges were given seats in the Senate so that the Senate became, in effect, a council of ministers. In adopting this design, Peter was following the Swedish administrative system.

Even before he reformed the central government, Peter tried to overhaul local administration. War had made this imperative because of the great demand for recruits and for the collection of taxes to finance campaigns. In 1708, he had divided the whole of Russia into eight (and subsequently eleven) governments. He appointed a governor for each to deal with all military and civil matters. The system, however, was not particularly effective. For the most part the governors stayed in Moscow and their orders were very often ignored.

Consequently, in 1719, Peter created fifty provinces, or *gubernias,* in place of the governments. This time the head of each area held the old title of *voivode*. Under each voivode were officials whose duties related to defense, justice, and other matters. This system also had grave weaknesses, the greatest of which was a lack of a proper code of law.

Since Peter was remote from his provinces, much information was withheld from him regarding the internal affairs of his states. Some attempt had already been made to revise the law, but the findings of a commission for that purpose had never been published. In 1720, there was an attempt to incorporate the Swedish code of law into national life, but it was unsuccessful. The Russian mind was as yet ill-tuned to such reform.

This serves to illustrate Peter's task in tackling the reactionary spirit and leading his country to maturity. Equally frustrating was the corruption and ignorance in civic duty. Education among officials was as scarce as dishonesty was widespread. It was easier to equip a regiment with loyal, efficient officers than it was to appoint administrators, who generally regarded office as a means of personal enrichment.

Staffs that were organized to try and trace corruption had to admit to failure. Dishonesty flourished even among the investigators. For instance, one man who had the power to expose even senators ended up on the wheel as punishment for extortion.

Peter had to warn his senators "not to handle the laws like games of cards." But his threats and entreaties were to little avail against the widespread graft. Even Menshikov was reproved and at times even thrashed for extorting.

But the time came when Peter resorted to more extreme measures than threats and beatings. The governor-general of Siberia was condemned to death. Two senators were flogged with the knout. A vice-chancellor was banished and a grand admiral heavily fined. As in the case with the code of law, Peter's attempts to end administrative corruption would finally meet with success, but not until many years had passed.

Peter gave some towns the right to set up municipal governments provided that they paid double taxes, but only eleven out of seventy communities gave what were regarded as honest returns. Eventually he changed the system. All the towns and their burgomasters came under a central body which met in Moscow.

Western ideas and methods did not root easily in Russia. The officials may have looked different in their new uniforms of German cloth, but in the main they did not change. As for the peasants, the changes only added to the confusion and the harassment.

Yet, taking the domestic scene as a whole, Peter's innovations were more fruitful than they seemed to be at first. Although his administrators were not averse to misappropriating money, they did try to promote education, rid the towns of crime, and help the country generally. And very often much of the money they collected dishonestly was taken from them in taxes. There were faults and weaknesses in Peter's new system, yet he left a firm basis on which to develop a sound administration.

Indeed, whatever criticism may be directed at Peter I, no one can deny the sincerity of his efforts to introduce a new governing class to ensure progress in Russia. There was, however, one glaring omission in his domestic reforms: he did little, if anything, to better the lives of the millions of ordinary people. Many of his subjects lived in dire poverty. Yet, like the wealthy classes, the common people were expected to serve the state. For many, this meant service in the army or labor in such projects as the construction of Petersburg, building harbors, ships, and canals. They worked under appalling conditions, often with little food.

It is curious that Peter did not display greater sympathy for the ordinary people. He himself possessed the common touch. He often worked with his hands among the people. He spurned luxury and was happy to live roughly in a simple hut. It was the factory and the hospital—not the art gallery—that attracted him.

The fact is that Peter was an organizer and a technician and not an advocate of social reform as we know it today. Even the boyars had been closer to the mass of the people than the Tsar was. The boyars had participated in the same religious customs as the common people and, in the main, had spent most of their time on the land among them. Now, engrossed in their official duties, the aristocrats sometimes went years without seeing their estates. When they did return it was clear that they had lost touch with their former way of life. A widening gap grew between the aristocracy and the people.

Some nobles kept many useless and idle servants on their estates, and the burden of maintaining them fell on the laboring classes. These servants often whiled away their time in the taverns drinking and gambling, and some resorted to crime when they were in need of money. Under the circumstances, it is not surprising that the once-close relationship between the nobility and the peasantry deteriorated.

The Tsar took no interest in the situation. To him the masses were no more than a source of recruits for war and money. To try and cope with the high costs of war, he increased the tax system. The ancient methods of taxing households proved inadequate, and in any event, many citizens evaded payment just by leaving their homes.

Peter employed idea men to work out new ways of extracting even more money from the already heavily burdened taxpayers. Because direct taxation was insufficient, indirect taxes were enforced. A dragoon tax was imposed on the clergy to buy cavalry horses. There were taxes on weights and measures, on horse collars, and on the wearing of leather boots. Funerals were taxed and so were marriages; "marriage," said Peter, "is a bit of luxury." Beards were already taxed, and those who wore them had to wear the traditional dress, which was also taxed. Cab fares were taxed, and so were hot baths, beds, milk, inns, mills, sheepskins, kitchen chimneys, hairdressings, bees, firewood, watermelons, cucumbers, and nuts.

By the end of Peter's reign, relatively few commodities had escaped the tax. Of all, salt yielded the most handsome returns.

By all accounts, taxation was not efficiently conducted, and the working classes suffered terribly under the resulting hardships. Indeed, the drain on the peasantry was enormous. They had to provide food for any military forces stationed near their homes. Often the troops forced inhabitants to leave their houses. Tax collectors lived at the expense of the people when they traveled. The peasants were also the prey of dishonest merchants who gave false weights and inaccurate measurements of cloth, and charged exorbitant prices. Furthermore, the peasants were the victims of their own ignorance. They clung to old-fashioned farming systems which were not very productive. Being unable to read or write, they had no way of knowing that crooked officials were issuing fake decrees to extract money or goods from them. Because so many of the rural people lived in a state of semistarvation, their numbers, originally in the millions, dwindled by about one-fifth, and in some regions by as much as one-third.

Hardship was not so acute in areas such as the Ukraine, but it was devastating in the more uncultivated provinces. Hatred festered—especially in places to which the Old Believers had fled and where members of the disbanded streltsy regiment and their families now lived and longed for revenge.

In 1705, much blood was shed in a riot in Astrakhan, then a hotbed of bandits and Volga pirates. A story circulated that the voivode of the Astrakhan area had forsaken Christ. All of these seething undercurrents burst through in the assassination of the voivode.

The new official was an Old Believer. The people of Astrakhan now rejected the authority of the Tsar. They appealed to the Cossacks and to the inhabitants of the Volga cities to unite with them and rise against Peter.

The insurrection could not be ignored. At the time, Peter was fighting the Swedes and, although he needed all his troops, he felt it necessary to send Sheremetev to the Volga. A mutiny in that area could possibly encourage disorder in the capital. Peter tried leniency, asking the mutineers to hand over their leaders in return for an amnesty.

Astrakhan continued to rebel. Peter's forces put down the rebellion, and hundreds of the defeated insurgents were tortured on the wheel, then executed. The ruthlessness of the Tsar was dramatized by the rafts that bore the gallows slowly down the Volga.

Under the restless Tsar, a new Russia was being molded in the furnace of war and domestic reform. Tragedy among the masses was the exacted price.

8

ARCHITECT OF FUTURE GLORY

Peter recognized three classes in Russia's social pattern: the aristocrats, the bourgeoisie, and the peasantry. The only thing these groups had in common was that they were all forced, directly or indirectly, to serve the state. Peter permitted the landowners to have power over the serfs and, in turn, the state to have control of the nobility. After his death, however, the nobles did manage to escape from some of their former obligations to the state. But they did not release their grip on the peasantry. The bitterness between the classes deepened. The result, years later, was a revolution that transformed the whole of Russia.

Peter tackled the problem of educating the people,

but his program did nothing for the peasants. It was too much of a task to educate the masses. Therefore, he concentrated on the aristocracy, the priests, and some of the merchants.

When Peter started his program, there were few schools in Russia. Credit must be given him for initiating the education of the Russian people. True, his system of education was limited, but he did create a framework on which universal popular education was later built.

In those days there was only one ecclesiastical school of any consequence: the Slav-Greco-Latin Academy, but even this institution had deteriorated. Peter was angry because the priests were illiterate and the one hundred and fifty scholars at the academy were left to their own devices. He did not wish to detract from the importance of religious instruction, but he impressed upon the Church authorities that the scholars must also be taught "to wage war, how to build, how to cure, and so become useful members of society."

The Tsar was conscious of the fact that his nation could never compete with the West until there were centers to train the technicians so lacking in Russia. There were few technical schools, but under Peter the number of textbooks began to increase. They were now coming from publishers in Amsterdam.

Peter enlisted his teachers from abroad, too. A man named Farquharson founded the first School of Mathematical Science and Navigation in Moscow in 1701.

Transferred to Petersburg four years later, the institute was rechristened the Naval Academy and became one of Russia's foremost centers of learning.

There were also other developments. The Livonian pastor who had once befriended Catherine founded what would eventually become a training center for diplomats. Students were trained in politics, modern languages, Latin, Hebrew, geography, riding, and dancing. Elsewhere, Jesuit fathers taught the sciences and the arts.

It was an erratic system of education, yet out of it grew a reputable school of medicine and centers for training officers in the engineers corps and the artillery.

This nucleus gradually extended its ramifications. Eventually, students from the Naval Academy went to every province. All had studied geography and geometry and were qualified to teach others. This was the way in which a dozen centers, inaugurated chiefly for the sons of military officers and the ecclesiastical class, were founded in the provinces in 1716. Another thirty would appear before Peter's reign ended. In addition, between 1721 and 1725, forty-six seminaries were established.

Unfortunately, the young student-nobles did not share the Tsar's enthusiasm for education. Discipline must have been extremely rigorous in these establishments. From all accounts, they were akin to prisons. At the Naval Academy, guards with whips stood at classroom doors to enforce discipline.

Peter also founded the Academy of Science, which

became of immense value to Russia. The idea of such an institution was the result of Peter's discussions with professors at the Sorbonne during his visit to Paris. While in Carlsbad, Peter had spent much time with Baron Gottfried von Leibnitz, the German scientist and philosopher. The Tsar had talked with him about mathematics and science and had asked him what should be done for the Russian people. "Build academies and universities in Petersburg, Moscow, Astrakhan, and Kiev," Leibnitz replied.

The German scientist had seen in the Tsar a man destined to bring greatness to his country. It is rather odd that although foreigners were quick to realize that Peter was the architect of Russia's future greatness, the Tsar's own people did not appreciate him. Similarly, although Protestants in Europe hailed him as a reformer in the manner of Luther, many of his own subjects condemned him as an Antichrist.

Accepting the advice of Baron Christian von Wolff, the German philosopher, Peter engaged fifteen German scientists for five years. On their arrival at Petersburg the scientists were astonished to find that they had no students to teach. Peter quickly formed a high school where pupils received a general education. However, the school was not opened until 1726, a year after the Tsar's death. It had a modest beginning with one hundred and twenty scholars, but they were the nucleus of today's educational system in Russia.

Another form of education which Peter introduced

was study abroad. It was the practice to send young students abroad in groups of one hundred and fifty. Initially they were sent to the shipyards and workshops of England and the Low Countries, but the scope of study was increased, and their visits were extended to other countries. Special attention was paid to the study of medicine. They learned the languages of the countries they visited. In Italy they studied architecture, in Holland painting. Paris was a center of study. Naval cadets were trained in France and in England.

By sending the young men of Russia abroad, Peter vastly improved the quality of his diplomats, administrators, and officers. All students were examined on their return home to see what they had learned. A rewarding future awaited those with skill, but many of the incompetent and indolent were assigned to menial tasks: for instance, working in the imperial kitchens or stables.

If there was any weakness in the system, it was a tendency among some students to taste too much of the pleasures of Western society. By so doing they also acquired some of the vices.

Some students caused trouble in the countries where they trained. In England, for instance, a number were imprisoned for debt. An Englishman who lost an eye in a brawl with a Russian claimed damages amounting to five hundred pounds sterling. In France the behavior of Russian cadets at Toulon prompted this comment: "They fight among themselves, give orders to the local authorities, and coarsely insult each other like the lowest of the low."

But on the whole, Peter's system produced excellent results. And even if the behavior of naval cadets sometimes caused anger abroad, the knowledge with which they returned to their homeland helped to build up Russian naval might.

Nothing is more fitting than to describe Peter as the father of the Russian navy. He was proud of his seamanship and thought himself to be a born sailor. He drank heavily in the tradition of a mariner, and even walked with his arms hanging at his sides like a Dutch seaman. Under his guidance Russian naval skill grew at a phenomenal rate.

At the outset of Peter's reign, the only Russians with experience on the sea were, more or less, the fishermen in the area of Archangel. Yet, in 1725, when his reign ended, Peter's squadrons consisted of 48 ships of the line and 787 galleys with crews totaling 28,000 men. Trained by foreign experts, the officer class expanded each year through promotions at the Naval Academy.

The story is told that Peter found water so repugnant that when his carriage crossed a millstream the curtains had to be drawn. This seems hard to believe, for no one can deny that from youth onward, shipbuilding and navigation obsessed him.

It has been suggested with some justification that Peter created a navy far out of proportion to Russia's needs. Perhaps a less grandiose sea force would have been enough to gain control of the Baltic coast. With ice closing the ports for half the year, Russia lacked a merchant navy and, therefore, seaborne trade. There were no cargoes to protect, and once Peter had conquered Swedish naval power a vast fleet was not essential. But the fact is that the Tsar aimed to make Russia the greatest European maritime power.

To build his fleet Peter was compelled to expend huge sums of money. Many thousands of men were removed from their normal duties and massed into a tremendous labor force to build ports or work on wharves. But much of this labor and money was wasted. For instance, the port construction near Taganrog on the Sea of Azov was eventually abandoned after the defeat at Prut. The Russians transferred the shipyards at Olonets to Petersburg, only to find that the Gulf of Finland at the new site was too shallow for launching larger vessels. Finally, when it was discovered that a site in Estonia met all requirements for the establishing of a port, storms wrecked the shipyards on which an enormous labor force had worked.

Peter's engineers and carpenters emulated the tough apprenticeship to which the Tsar had subjected himself in England and Holland. English specialists were so helpful that the British government grew worried over the growth of Russian maritime power. The Tsar himself was favorably impressed by the standard of French shipbuilding. In fact, the vessel that appealed to him most was the French frigate *Le Ferme*.

It was the smaller galleys, not so much the powerful

squadrons, which allowed Peter to gain control of the Baltic. From the Greeks and Dalmatians who visited Russia during Peter's first campaign against the Turks, the Tsar derived the idea and the technique to build these small vessels. They were navigable both in big rivers and at sea. When infantrymen worked the oars, the galleys—which surprised the Swedes—were ideal both for landing on coasts and for boarding ships. Even infantry captains could navigate these very mobile craft.

Although the naval actions were of the utmost significance, it was on the battlefield that the great issues were decided. And although Peter liked to think of himself as a son of the sea, it was in his military campaigns that he really excelled. He inspired his nation to military glory. Up to the time of his reign Russia had depended on foreign mercenaries. Peter taught his people to rely on their own resources. Charles XII of Sweden had at first treated the Russian army with contempt, but he lived to respect it and to see it destroy his power.

In the beginning Peter had fielded the undisciplined force that suffered the inglorious rout at Narva; by the end of his life, he commanded a powerful and efficient regular army. In addition to the two regiments of the Guard, he had fifty regiments of infantry; thirty of dragoons; units of Hussars, sixty-seven garrisons, and six militia regiments. This constituted a regular army of some 200,000 men.

Russia possessed a wealth of manpower. Previous

tsars had also put huge armies in the field, but never before had the Russian military been invested with such fine equipment or such brilliant training. Whitworth, the English ambassador, gave unstinted praise to the Russian foot soldiers who "marched in perfect order, bearing cold, hunger, and every kind of fatigue without difficulty, and the officers themselves were in wonderment in face of the zeal and devotion of their subordinates. As for the artillery, foreign experts say that they have never seen any other nation handle cannon and mortars with such skill."

A mercenary named Manstein claimed that "nowhere in Europe is there an artillery comparable to that of the Russians, still less one that can surpass it."

Pleyer, the German diplomat, referred directly to Peter as the architect of this new army. He wrote: "One cannot but marvel to what point, thanks to the tireless efforts of the Tsar, the soldiers have attained perfection in their exercises, with what discipline they execute the orders of their officers, with what courage they conduct themselves in battle."

Not many years after the defeat at Narva, the Russians had three thousand pieces of field artillery, and the figure continued to rise. Before he died, Peter knew that his country was strongly defended by his imperial army. There was a general repository for heavy ordnance in the capital. The artillery trains of Petersburg, Narva, and Briansk each numbered 204 cannon and 74 mortars, and every infantry battalion and each regiment of dragoons possessed two field guns.

If there was any weakness in any part of the army, it was in the corps of engineers. The Russians were not as successful in engineering as in artillery.

Narva had taught Peter that training was not everything; his troops must also be adequately equipped. He obviously made sure of this. According to Pleyer: "Their clothing is supplied by Russian industry. An excellent factory produces the cloth; they lack neither hats nor woollen stockings; shoes, boots and linen for their shirts are imported, through Kief, from various centres. . . . The powdermills stand idle because enormous stocks are available in spite of all that is wasted at military exercises and during the Imperial banquets. The Tsar gets a splendid iron from Siberia, very workable, which they use for gun barrels: no better could be found in Sweden. The hard iron of Tula and Olonets, used in the manufacture of bombs and grenades, is of far better quality than anyone could find elsewhere and possesses the advantage of shattering into a thousand splinters on explosion. As for sulphur and saltpetre, plenty of that is to be had in the Ukraine. Nothing is lacking, then, for the conduct of a long war."

Peter's army was also distinguished from any previous Russian force by its high morale. The Tsar inspired this spirit among his troops by personal example. He was continually in the thick of fighting, mixing with the ordinary soldiers and encouraging them with his willingness to sacrifice himself, if necessary.

Peter created a true class of military professionals.

The honors and rewards he bestowed on those who distinguished themselves show the importance he attached to the officer class. For example, after the conquest of Azov, Peter made Lefort the vice-duke of Novgorod. He gave him a number of villages and an estate near Moscow with two hundred slaves, many pieces of figured cloth, a sable robe, and a golden vase with an engraving of the Tsar's name. To the Scotsman Gordon on the same occasion, he gave a medal worth six ducats, a gold cup, a valuable sable robe, and an estate with ninety slaves.

To those who exhibited cowardice Peter was ruthless, inflicting the harshest penalities. Some writers have emphasized his streak of cruelty without acknowledging his humanitarianism. But in the Military Regulations, which set the code of conduct for his army, he expressed as his aim to win battles "with the least costly effort and without too much bloodshed." Although he did not always adhere to this rule himself, he warned his soldiers of the severe punishment that awaited them should they offend peaceable residents "not only in their own country or in allied or neutral countries, but also in enemy territory."

The changed pattern of the Russian army was reflected in its leading officers. Initially, Peter had relied on foreign mercenaries. But at the end of his reign, the number of Russian officers far exceeded the foreign experts.

Peter also appointed a Russian as his commissioner-general for the armies. Virtually all the brigadiers and colonels were Russian, and this officer class would be the power in the Russian army for generations to come—indeed, right to the end of tsarist rule.

9

TRADE AND INDUSTRY AWAKEN

The formation and maintenance of Russia's new regular army, plus the burden of war, imposed tremendous strains on the country's economy. Although the Northern War had been a serious drain on the public purse, Peter emerged from the hostilities without incurring a single debt. Furthermore, at the time of his death he was solvent to the extent of seven million rubles.

Peter knew that to achieve international power Russia must be strong not only in a military sense but also in an economic one. Therefore, he stimulated trade. In his later years, revenue from the export of Russian goods rose to twice the amount of imports.

A treaty developed trade with Persia. Commerce was renewed with China and Central Asia, and traffic was made easier with the West now that Russia had Baltic outlets. Peter had developed Archangel but then allowed it to decay. In 1693, a total of 29 foreign merchants had offices in the port. This number increased to 149 warehouses and offices in 1702. Fourteen years later, the number had grown to 233.

Peter, however, was a realist. Although he had founded his navy at Archangel, and had developed the port, to some extent Archangel had been only a playground. The Baltic offered greater opportunities for trade, and Peter did not allow sentiment to cloud his vision. In 1722, the authorities were stopped from importing to Archangel more than was required for local needs. From that time on, the port was ruined as a trading center.

To develop trade elsewhere, Peter encouraged Russian businessmen to deal with the West, thus ending the monopoly of the foreign merchants. The Tsar even subsidized companies who showed initiative in this direction. Although the ventures were not always profitable, at least Russian commerce was awakened to more adventurous enterprises.

Two things were needed for the further development of trade in Russia: more capital and adequate roads. To safeguard the merchants, Peter, like previous tsars, forbade aliens from trading in the interior of the country or selling their goods beyond the ports of disembarkation.

Improved communications were necessary, too, but this presented an even more difficult problem, both financially and economically. The Tsar thought that the answer lay in canals. He conceived the idea of a waterway joining the Don and Volga rivers, an ambitious project which was completed by the Russians only at the end of World War II.

However, during Peter's reign, the Vishny-Volotshok canal between the Volga and the Neva rivers was constructed, extending marine transport to Lake Ladoga. Because of the hazards of these stormy waters, a second canal, sixty-two miles long, was cut on the fringe of the lake. With customary zeal Peter accompanied the engineers when the marshy terrain was explored.

Whereas Peter left his imprint on industry—to the point that, directly or indirectly, the foundation for much of the Soviets' present-day progress can be attributed to him—he did little for agriculture. He saw that flax, hemp, tobacco, and medicinal herbs were cultivated; that vines were planted on the shores of the Caspian Sea; and that Merino sheep and purebred cattle were reared. But that was virtually all he did.

The Tsar's paramount interest in the earth was the extraction of its riches. Today the Soviet Union is self-sufficient in this area, largely due to the rich mineral wealth of Siberia. Peter guessed rightly that Russian soil possessed latent wealth. Enough minerals had been located there "that they ought to suffice until the end of the world."

Peter wrote: "Russia is more favored than any other

state by its resources in metal and mineral which no one so far has sought to exploit."

That is why Peter differed from his predecessors. He was conscious of "a great gift granted by God" to Russia, and he made use of it. At first, it was the war that necessitated the exploitation of natural resources. For instance, cannon were seriously needed by the army. Encouraged by the Tsar, the cannon-smith Demidov founded the first ironworks at Nevyansk. In so doing this energetic craftsman became a millionaire.

But Peter's influence was much wider, resulting in the huge iron industry in the Urals. Also because of the army's needs, he stimulated the production of coarse cloth and heavy boots. Manufacturing was expanded in other areas. In Peter's lifetime not only iron but also silver and copper were exploited.

At the end of his reign new enterprises totaled 221. Ironworks and arsenals numbered 86. Prominent, too, in the economy were 15 cloth mills, a smaller number of woolen mills, 14 leatherworks, 9 silk mills and tapestry workshops.

Klyuchevsky, the historian, sums up the industrial scene: "To foreign eyes the whole of Russia in the reign of Peter the Great appeared a vast workshop where hidden treasure was being extracted from the earth, where the air re-echoed everywhere to the clang of hammers and axes, and where on every side learned specialists and skillful workmen were to be seen flocking in with their books, tools, and instruments."

One remaining obstacle to progress was the apathy

among Russians. The affluent would risk heavy penalties by hiding their money or investing it in foreign banks instead of risking it in new domestic ventures. To combat this reluctance, capitalists were forced, by means of decrees, to erect factories and start trading companies.

It took time to build up markets for Russian manufactures. There was no shortage of foreign traders willing to buy the raw materials, but the same enthusiasm was not shown for the products. Even home sales of woolen cloth and linen were limited. It should be pointed out, however, that the standard of production was not always high. But Peter knew that in time all this would change.

He demonstrated his belief when his sister-in-law gave him a piece of poor-quality cloth. It had been made by a man named Milyutin, who had taught himself weaving. Peter encouraged the weaver, and the man developed in skill to become one of the finest textile manufacturers of his day.

In founding his regular army, Peter first engaged foreign officers for the highest ranks. Similarly, in the pioneer days of industry, he often had to look abroad for people who could accept managerial responsibility. This definitely applied to the heavier industries.

Problems also often arose through a shortage of unskilled workers. Forced labor was the main answer. Another source was Swedish prisoners of war and people who would otherwise have been imprisoned. Some twenty-five thousand peasants on the estates were directed to the metalworks in the Urals, and about twelve thousand for similar duties at Olonets. When it was clear that only a small percentage of the labor force would consist of freemen, managements and merchants were empowered, in 1721, to buy serfs from the landed gentry.

The lack of desire to work in industry is easily explained. Payment was dreadfully poor and sometimes wages were never even paid. In the summer the people worked for thirteen hours daily, and for almost that long in winter. In the living quarters, hygiene and cleanliness were often ignored. It was not surprising, therefore, that these conditions bred riots and strikes. The individual was of no concern. He was sacrificed on the altar of the new industries in the interests of the state. But out of this wretched existence was laid the structure of Russian industrial power.

10

THE HOLY SYNOD

Because of the general resentment toward change, Peter could never have avoided anger and criticism in any sphere of Russian life, even if he had been the kindest of monarchs. And this was certainly true in ecclesiastical matters. It is also true that Russia never could have progressed or competed with other nations had not Peter reformed the Church.

Over the years the Church had grown rich and powerful. Due to gifts from the more prominent faithful—usually in the form of estates—the Church had become the country's biggest landowner. Thus, for years more and more authority was vested in the Patriarch.

In fact, the Patriarch enjoyed his own sovereign power which, if anything, was even greater than that of the Tsar himself. The Tsar derived much of his authority from the national acceptance that he was the sole defender of the true faith. The Palm Sunday procession in the streets of Moscow, when the Tsar, on foot, led the horse carrying the Patriarch rather illustrates the relationship between head of state and head of the Church.

Unfortunately, the Church concentrated on feasts and rituals. Largely because the priests were uneducated, it failed to instruct the people and, therefore, hindered progress. For instance, at the time when only a few aliens practiced medicine in Moscow, these doctors were constantly harassed and ridiculed by the ignorant priests.

By Peter's standards, the Church was often reactionary and narrow in outlook. In his will, the Patriarch Joachim had even besought Peter to get rid of the "heretic" churches in the foreign quarter; to execute anyone who tried to convert; to ban the discussion of religious problems; and to rid Russia of foreign soldiers.

Patriarch Adrian was appointed after Joachim's death, and for the rest of his life Adrian tried to obstruct any innovation by the Tsar. It is understandable that Peter lessened the Patriarchate's influence after Adrian died.

But the greatest Church reform, the creation of a

Holy Synod, or governing body, occurred a few years before the end of Peter's reign. The man who contributed most to this change was Feofan Prokopovich, a clergyman with a Western outlook. In 1719 and 1720, he published new regulations of ecclesiastical procedure and behavior, and was instrumental in bringing about the Synod in 1721.

The ecclesiastical regulations explain the purpose of the reform: "Government of the Church by the Synod will spare the State troubles and doubts that are inevitable when the Church is subject to a single head. Simple people do not know the difference between ecclesiastical power and temporal power: impressed by the glories and honors of the Supreme Priest he thinks that the latter is another Sovereign equal to the Ruler or even stronger than he. If that is the opinion of the people, what will happen if an ambitious cleric comes to stir up strife? On the other hand, if the people see that rule by Synod is introduced by a decree of the Sovereign and by the decision of the Senate, they will submit meekly and will lose any hope of support from the clergy in their revolts. The perfect union of the two authorities is salutary in the first place for the Church itself."

From this, it is clear that Peter was pruning the Church of much of its former power. He certainly had no intention of allowing a Russian pope to overrule or challenge his authority. This makes him quite different from his predecessors. The introduction of the Holy

Synod was as eventful in Russia as was the Reformation in Europe, for until Peter's reign the Church had figured prominently in the nation's life. Spiritual power had equaled secular power. What was more distasteful to Peter was that the Church, which had such a marked influence on the people, championed the traditions he wished to destroy.

It was the Church that clung to the ancient calendar and the out-of-date alphabet. It insisted on beards; upheld the wearing of medieval dress; and taught that women should remain in the background of society. It bred superstition and mystery, and inspired the belief that the Patriarch, being closer to God than the Tsar by nature of his office, had both greater wisdom and greater authority.

The ecclesiastical regulations of Prokopovich, who was archbishop of Novgorod, attacked all these ideas. Like Peter, Prokopovich was a realist. He loathed Roman Catholicism, but he was enthusiastic about the writings of Luther and Calvin. The setting up of a Holy Synod was influenced indirectly by the Protestant churches of the West.

To a great extent the Holy Synod was akin to an ecclesiastical committee founded to carry out the Tsar's will. Peter maintained the right to appoint the members, who now directed all Church matters, such as the nomination of bishops; the administration of ecclesiastical estates; maintenance of doctrine; jurisdiction of the clergy; matrimonial suits; supervision of parish schools;

management of seminaries; publication of textbooks; censorship of books; and relief for the poor, the sick, and the orphans.

The Holy Synod, composed of eleven members, started to function on February 14, 1721. Stephen Yavorsky was president, but Prokopovich was the dominant force. He and Theodosy Yanovsky were the vice-presidents, and there were four counselors who were in charge of the chief monasteries and the assessors. A procurator was appointed to be "the eyes of the Tsar" at meetings of the Synod, but his duties were no more than that of reporter to Peter. Actually, the Synod, whose members resided and convened in Petersburg, dealt directly with the Tsar.

No one could question the Synod's decisions except Peter. Indeed, as in the case of the Senate, the Holy Synod received its authority from the Tsar. At no time was it popular either with the clergy or the people. But Peter did not seek to be popular. His objective was to raise his country from medieval sloth to modern efficiency. To accomplish this he did not appeal to the nation, but ruthlessly imposed his will upon it.

When Yavorsky died in 1722, no one was named to succeed him. Yanovsky filled the president's duties until he fell into disfavor with Peter, who had him banished to a monastery. Prokopovich was more subtle. He lauded Peter as the "supreme pastor" and continued to be the sovereign's spiritual adviser.

It must be emphasized that, although Peter reformed

the Orthodox Church and deprived it of much of its independence, eventually the clergy tended to be servile to the tsarist regime. It is no exaggeration to say that Peter founded an institution which was not unlike the Protestant consistories, and wished to use the Church for the good of his country. He wanted it to be an instrument to help educate the ignorant masses and to do away with their superstitions.

Peter also wanted less ignorance, corruption, and indolence in the Church itself. He objected to uneducated men entering the priesthood; under Peter, candidates had to be at least thirty years old. There was much scope for improving the standard of the clergy. In the country it was quite common to see a slovenly, drunken priest. Even divine service was celebrated no more than a few times each year.

Priests who had no parish were now liable to tax. In Peter's view the monasteries should cease to acquire wealth, and so he banned the further purchase of land and also interfered with their income. Revenue was to be used not only for the maintenance of monks and priests, but also for social activities. No new religious centers were to be built, and even in the existing ones the number of monks was restricted. To repair monastery walls, old gravestones were to be used. Nuns were charged with the care of the sick and the wounded.

Peter was unique among the monarchs of his time in that he advocated religious tolerance. Yet his attitude here seems somewhat irregular. The foreign elements in Russia were permitted to construct their own churches. Mixed marriages and conversions were also allowed. De la Vie, the French diplomat, commented in 1717: "Liberty of conscience is absolute here since the Tsar permits doctors of religions differing from his own to make proselytes [converts]."

But at the same time Peter forbade the right of entry to Jewish aliens. And although he was willing to grant freedom of worship, the prospect of unity among the churches was distasteful to him. During his visit to France he had been asked at the Sorbonne if he would unite the churches of the East and West. For political reasons, he agreed to consider this question, but nothing came of it.

There were times when Peter acted as though he did wish to effect a reunion but, in fact, he regarded himself as the defender of the true faith. To submit to the Pope was out of the question. However, the Orthodox Church and the Roman Catholics did have dealings with each other. No objection was made to the monks of Catholic orders settling in Russia, and Peter tried to protect members of the Orthodox Church from Catholic persecution in Poland.

In his own country, Peter ordered an end to persecution of the Old Believers, but he insisted that they wear a red square of cloth fringed with yellow.

11

WINDOW ON THE WEST

Peter I did many unpopular things, but the one that evoked the greatest hostility was his decision to transfer the seat of government from Moscow to Petersburg. The city that had risen out of the northern marshes became the capital of the empire. It was an incredible accomplishment, at a time of warfare in territory that Peter was not sure of retaining.

To leave Moscow, with its many established government buildings, in favor of a wilderness was in itself audacious. But to Peter, Moscow—four hundred miles from Petersburg—was much too steeped in the traditions he wished to destroy. His new city was farther away from the heart of Russia, but closer to Europe and the culture which he admired. In short, Petersburg was a window on the West.

At the outset, the city was christened Petropolis, then Piterburkh, and finally St. Petersburg. Peter's dream capital had begun as a fortification. In a sense it was the product of sweat, toil, and human misery, for owing to the scarcity of picks, shovels, and other tools the first foundations were dug mostly with bare hands. Swedish and Livonian prisoners augmented the many thousands of workmen who were drafted from most parts of Russia. Soil had to be carried over long distances in sacks or in the laborers' coats. There were not enough wheelbarrows and never enough food and shelter for this gargantuan work force.

Manpower was plentiful and labor was compulsory. For the rest of his reign Peter ensured a flow of artisans from the provinces to his capital. Every fifth or tenth dwelling yielded one worker for several months. For years masons, ironsmiths, clockmakers, and others reported each month to the authorities in Petersburg. Evasion of service drew severe punishment.

The initial work at Petersburg was supervised by Peter himself. To create a nucleus for his future city, the Tsar ordered merchants and others to move there. When boyars and other members of the aristocracy arrived with their enormous retinues, the population grew quickly.

To some extent Petersburg was a heyday for opportunists. Weber, a diplomat and a contemporary chronicler, wrote: "The merchants and the professionals turned this new place, where everything was so dear, to good account."

One of the amazing facets of Peter's character was that, even though uncertain that he could retain the surrounding land, he threw himself exuberantly into the construction of this northern center. Had he already decided to make the city his capital, his energy could have been appreciated, but at the beginning there was no such decision. At no time did he issue a decree ordering that the capital be transferred. It was a decision that gradually took shape, gathering momentum after Poltava and becoming a reality after victories at Viborg and Riga—"two cushions," said Peter, "on which Petersburg can rest in complete tranquillity."

In 1703, Peter led a fleet of six vessels from Olonets to Petersburg. It was the birth of Petersburg as a port. The first foreign vessel to arrive there was a ship flying the Dutch flag. Peter celebrated the occasion on board. After presenting five hundred ducats to the skipper and gifts to the crew, he entertained them in Menshikov's home.

Trade swelled to the point that Petersburg vied with Archangel and eventually eclipsed its rival. This was due to three factors. First, Petersburg was better placed geographically for trade; second, Peter banned the export of goods via the White Sea except for local merchandise; and third, Petersburg, chosen as a bastion of defense, became the key center for naval administration.

Even while war operations were in progress Peter

spent much time at Petersburg. After the Poltava celebrations he left the Kremlin. His new city would be different; it would avoid the ornate. Petersburg would be classical in style—the Amsterdam of the north. Moscow was too old-fashioned and unsuited to him. He much preferred his small, simple home with casement windows, which was built along Dutch lines. Foreign ships' captains, arriving in Petersburg for the first time, were amazed to find that the ruler of the world's greatest empire lived so modestly.

Early in 1708, Peter lay ill at his capital and was temporarily out of the war with Charles. He sent a messenger to his sister Natalia, his two half-sisters, and the two dowager Tsaritsas, asking them to visit him in the spring. Also invited were leading aristocrats, high officials, and rich merchants. The guests were not pleased with the "invitations."

Whitworth, the English ambassador, recorded: "This journey will be long and very costly for all the nobility, for time was not allowed them to send to their villages for provisions, and they are obliged to buy most of these on the way for ready money. They have taken with them huge quantities of luggage because it is said that nothing can be bought on the spot. They go with heavy hearts, but no one is allowed to excuse himself by pleading age or illness."

In the early stages, most of the buildings in Petersburg were made of wood but this was largely changed, especially after 1710. In that year fire destroyed many of the buildings. Panic broke out and in the subsequent chaos some of the laborers plundered the shops. Displaying his usual ferocity at such times, Peter had the culprits hanged from hastily erected scaffolds in the marketplace.

The lesson learned from this disaster was that stone and brick must be used in the construction of buildings. However, there was a shortage of both masons and materials. But Peter was not to be obstructed. Petersburg—his "paradise"—must be completed. Therefore, in October, 1714, he forbade the erection of stone structures elsewhere in Russia for a number of years—"in pain of confiscation of goods and of exile." Building was stopped even in Moscow.

Masons trekked northward to join the multitude of workers who labored even at night by the glow of pitch and wood fires. Amid the noise and the confusion, the city rose. And watching it grow was the giant foreman—the Tsar, who strode among the workers in top boots and reindeer skin, with a cudgel that he never hesitated to use.

The immensity and imaginative scope of Peter's new city attracted architects from Italy, Germany, Holland, and France. The first architect to the Russian court was an Italian, Trezzini. He planned the houses of affluent citizens until two Germans, Schädel and Schlüter, achieved popularity. In 1716, a Frenchman named Leblond was entrusted with the general civic design.

Toward the end of Peter's life, the Cathedral of Saints Peter and Paul, where from now on the Romanov tsars and princes would be buried, dominated the Petersburg skyline. Near it was the somber fortress for state prisoners. There was also the Church of the Holy Trinity where Peter worshiped, the chancellery, the hospital, the printing press, and the mint.

There were many other buildings and shops. Not far from Menshikov's palace stood the Twelve Colleges, a building designed to accommodate the departments of the central administration.

Petersburg was never planned as a single, unified project. Instead, the pattern was casual, a series of unrelated designs. Because of this, much time, effort, and materials were wasted. For instance, Peter, dealing with the two large islands in the Neva delta, attempted first to develop the one nearer the right bank of the river, but the flooding was so extensive that the main structures, such as the palaces and cathedrals, eventually had to be erected on the left bank.

Toward the end of his reign the Tsar was obsessed with the desire to imitate Venice. There would be canals in place of streets, but this meant transferring the city to lower land—to the Isle Basil, closest to the river mouth.

At Peter's request Leblond drew up a scheme to drain the area by a network of canals big enough to take vessels. Along with this striking pattern of land and water, Peter visualized his Imperial Palace in the midst of gardens. Some of the work was accomplished, but the canals silted up and became useless for transport. The transfer of the city, therefore, was not undertaken. Indeed, many of Peter's ideas never materialized. In fact, although he originally conceived of Petersburg entirely as an island city, its imposing houses spread along the southern bank of the Neva. Farther downstream were the admiralty buildings. Here were offices, workrooms for the draftsmen, forges, workmen's quarters, and warehouses for storing sails, ropes, and other materials. Here, too, was the shipyard.

When he was in Petersburg the Tsar supervised activities in the shipyard, even wielding an ax with skill. Peter was proud of the admiralty and often entertained his guests there, behaving as if he were on board ship.

There was a suggestion of the navy even at Peter's winter palace. At the main entrance two columns were surmounted by the prow of a ship. Except for the large state room, apartments were for the most part rather small. Peter liked it that way. And although the ceilings were high so that the palace was in keeping with nearby residences, lower artificial ceilings were constructed in the living rooms to achieve a more homelike effect.

For his summer palace, Peter chose a site on the bank of a tributary of the Neva. It consisted of three buildings, and the main one has survived. It still contains the Tsar's furniture and the cabinetmaker's lathe with which he made cupboards in the Dutch style. But gone are the gardens—with the flower beds, grottoes, and fountains—which were inspired by the park at Versailles.

It was to be expected that the mansions of the dignitaries would be situated between the Tsar's residences. One house was occupied by Count Bruce, grand master of artillery and commandant of Petersburg, but eventually was taken over by the Holy Synod. Also near the summer palace was the arsenal where cannon were cast, and the Kunstkammer, a scientific museum which possessed a valuable natural-history collection. The surrounding countryside was dotted with chalets.

The people of consequence—and certainly those who dealt with the Tsar—were reached by boat in the summer or by river sledge in the winter. Most of the other citizens lived in the marshlands. All Russian landowners who owned estates of more than seven hundred serfs were ordered to erect stone houses in Petersburg.

Peter strengthened the continuation of Petersburg by developing industry. Silk mills, rope factories, brick-works, factories for linen, biscuits, and other industries were established. French workers from the factories of Beauvais and Gobelin wove carpets, tapestries, screens, and seats. Tar and gunpowder works and a sugar refinery were in operation.

The future of Petersburg seemed assured. The creation of a garrison port—Kronstadt—approaching the Gulf of Finland further safeguarded Peter's capital. A channel was defended on both sides by three hundred cannon. On the right was Croonsloot, a war tower for the garrison, and on the left lay the island of Retusaari. A decade earlier, there had been only woods and a sprinkling of fishermen's dwellings in this spot, but now there were mansions.

In 1721, de Campredon, the French diplomat, wrote: "A great canal, about half a league long, is being dug which will traverse the whole island and will be faced with stone: at the end there will be six docks for refitting vessels under a stone arch one hundred feet in height and surmounted by a great tower with a beacon light. There are two harbors, one formed for ships of war, the other for merchant vessels, enclosed by piles on which a fortress of fifteen bastions is to be erected. The foundations are laid: twenty thousand men will be working there next spring and everything should be completed in two or three years more. It will be one of the finest ports in Europe."

The forges of Systerbeck on the north shore of the gulf yielded the anchors and other items for warships at Kronstadt, as well as guns, pistols, and swords for the army. The Russians were gaining a wide reputation for the skill shown in their foundries.

Peter could see Kronstadt from his home at Peterhof —eighteen miles west of the capital—to which he retired for pleasure. From the sea a canal faced with stone ran in a straight line to Peter's estate. Fountains and statues decorated the gardens. The Tsar's following and his staff occupied the ground floor; the upper floor comprised his apartments. These have been described as small but elegant, and adorned with beautiful furniture and paintings.

Peter's pavilion, known as Mon Plaisir, was built right at the fringe of the gulf. Again, the architectural style resembled that of Holland. From his narrow white-walled bedroom Peter could gaze on a scene which always pleased him: heavily fortified Kronstadt with its ships. A favorite pastime was to conduct guests through his gardens to a pavilion called Marly in which were hung exquisite paintings.

Fire caused terrible tragedies in Petersburg. Like his officials, Peter received a salary for duties as a fireman. By helping to fight these blazes, Peter aimed to instill a sense of fire consciousness into the residents and to learn how to tackle this danger more efficiently. The Danish diplomat Juel relates: "I have often seen him arrive first at a fire, with a small hose in his sledge. He takes part in all the business of life-saving and as his intelligence is extraordinarily quick, he sees at once what must be done to extinguish the fire: he goes up to the roof; he goes to all the worst danger points; he incites nobles as well as common people to help in the struggle and does not pause until the fire is put out. In this way he averts great calamities."

Apparently when the Tsar was absent the story was quite different. "The people," Juel went on, "watch the fires with indifference and do nothing to help extinguish them: it is vain to lecture them or even to offer them money. They merely wait for a chance to steal something. . . ."

The flooding of the Neva River and vicious gales also contributed to the citizens' terrors. Nearly every year the river overflowed into homes. Accounts by foreign observers testify to the ferocity of the elements in Petersburg. During a gale in November, 1721, even bridges were blown away. De la Vie wrote: "The storm blew with such terrible violence that if it had gone on for two hours more this town would have been completely ruined. The damage caused is beyond words: not a single house is left that has not had its share. Losses are calculated at two or three million rubles. . . . It will be enough if I say that the Tsar, like another Philip of Spain, made the greatness of his soul clear by his tranquillity."

Fire and flooded homes—and sometimes the subsequent loss of livestock and merchandise—were not the only dangers besetting the citizens. In the winter they faced the threat of hungry wolves. During darkness robbers and burglars preyed on them. In the city's inadequate, and in places nonexistent, street lighting, crime was commonplace. The number of police was far too small in relation to the population.

Many citizens in Petersburg regarded the new capital as a piece of tsarist folly and bemoaned their fate. Peter's city did not endear itself to them. For the nation as a whole, Moscow still remained the pivot of religious, economic, and cultural activity. Many people in the country hoped and prophesied that after Peter's death Petersburg would decay.

But the prophecies were wrong. Petersburg remained the capital of tsarist Russia for two centuries. Its name was changed in 1914 to Petrograd, the Russian form of

12

AN EXAMPLE TO OTHERS

Whatever criticisms may be leveled against Peter, it cannot be said that he lived in the luxury normally expected of the ruler of an empire. Indeed, some of his friends lived much more lavishly and in greater splendor.

Perhaps never before had a tsar been so close to the ordinary people. There was no aloofness in his relationships. He would play chess with common folk, and mix with all levels of society. His table manners were no better than those of the crudest worker. Dispensing with knife and fork, he would hold a hot piece of meat in his bare hands. Indeed, to Peter, manners in general were a waste of time. If he was warm, he would remove his caftan no matter who was with him.

Yet it is ironic that monarch and nation did not understand each other. His predecessors, the essence of grandeur in comparison with Peter, had been aloof from the mass of the people, appearing before them somewhat rarely—chiefly on ceremonial occasions. At such times, the sovereign was surrounded by so many dignitaries that often he himself could not be seen.

Peter was different. Usually smoking a pipe, he moved freely among his subjects and was more inelegant than many of them. In Petersburg he often wore a simple green tunic with a sword knot of black leather. Another favored attire was a Dutch sailor jacket. On ceremonial occasions he would wear a red uniform with a small Swedish-type collar. Typical was the time in Copenhagen when he was seen in a green cap, a brown overcoat with horn buttons, a woolen waistcoat, cravat, and extremely tight knee breeches. He also wore a nightcap and an ancient dressing gown of Chinese cotton when he received his visitors. Sometimes he would appear in shirtsleeves.

Wigs did not appeal to him. If he suddenly felt the need for one, he would quite likely grab it from somebody's head. In the same way he would take the nearest carriage if his own was not readily available.

Under the circumstances, it is ironic that Peter should have attached such importance to what his subjects wore. Eventually, he insisted that they cast off the medieval caftan in favor of Western dress. Yet he himself would wear darned socks and clothes that were nearly threadbare.

Peter I was a unique personality by any standard. This was symbolized by his enormous height; at six feet eight he was much taller than most men. His face, too, was arresting, being large and ruddy. The dark eyes were piercing and the forehead was broad. When he walked he took huge strides, so that it was difficult to keep pace with him. The movement of his hands was jerky, implying the restlessness of his nature. Actually, he could not stay still for long. His physical strength was prodigious; he could break horseshoes with his bare hands.

Peter was one of the most forceful men in history. He saw himself as a barbarian ruling a nation of barbarians on the fringe of a civilization in which European nations had a marked superiority. The victim of a savage temper and hysterical outbursts, he remained uncivilized throughout his life. Yet he allowed nothing to deter him from civilizing his people. Only a colossus could have accomplished as much. True, as an autocrat, he possessed unlimited power, yet it is to his credit that he never used that power for selfish gain. His sole aim was to exalt Russia, and his courage and vision were directed to that end.

What is striking about his personality are the contradictions. Peter was blunt in manner and despotic, and although it was said that he would not harm a bird, he could be extremely cruel to human beings, even killing in a fit of anger. There were times of hysterical violence, yet he could also display kindness and consideration. And if he drove others to achieve great physical tasks, he himself set the example.

Indeed, his capacity for work was fantastic. He would toil for many hours without rest and he could engage in feasting for just as long. The heavy drinking doubtless impaired his health. However, no matter how long he drank, Peter did not lose control of his wits. It has been suggested that he encouraged—and even compelled—others to drink in order to find out what lurked in their minds. A custom which almost became a ritual was his glass of vodka or schnapps at midday. This he called "the admiral's hour."

Part of his character was of a simplicity which, to some extent, seems rather attractive in such an unusual and vigorous personality. As we have seen, he preferred a homey intimacy to the grandeur of palace rooms. While in France, for instance, he found the ceiling of the room in which he was staying much too high. And so he had a lower ceiling made from a sail.

Apart from his simplicity, Peter was unpretentious, detesting liars and braggarts. His plain tastes extended to food. One hears much about the great feasts, yet he was content with stews, vegetables, and whole-wheat bread. He favored cheese and fruit in place of sweets. As often as not he would dine alone. He scoffed at the ceremonial banquets which, he suggested, had been introduced "to punish the great and rich for their sins." When duty compelled him to attend these affairs, he often avoided the place of honor, choosing instead a less conspicuous seat so that he could leave when he became bored. Being a man of action, he was too impatient to sit still for any length of time. At banquets it was common to see him suddenly quit his chair and exercise his legs in an adjoining room. Sometimes he would leave to catch up on some sleep, ordering his guests to remain seated until he returned.

Peter had little interest in official receptions. Such ceremonies seemed to affect him adversely. Usually a commanding personality, he was, under these circumstances, embarrassed and confused; he perspired and breathed heavily. Often, as soon as the ceremony was over, he would change his clothes and seek more congenial company—a foreign merchant, perhaps—or he would devote himself to a craft.

He disliked the pomp and etiquette of the court and was quite out of keeping with the normal image of a sovereign. Nations generally regarded—and usually preferred—their monarchs to be the center of magnificence, someone of regal bearing, elegant gesture, and the epitome of refinement. Peter I was quite the reverse. He shunned and disliked anything that smacked of the majestic. He was often uncouth—sometimes his behavior was in the worst possible taste—and his language and humor echoed the barrack room and the tavern.

Rather than glorify his status as Tsar, he did much to minimize it. A law introduced on December 11, 1701, forbade his people to kneel and prostrate themselves in his presence or raise their hats when passing his palace. Characteristically he commented: "What difference can there be between God and the Tsar, if both are venerated in the same fashion? Less abasement, more zeal, and fidelity, toward me and toward the State—these are the real honors I seek."

In this last sentence is the objective for which Peter always strove. No matter how much he was attracted by the West in general, and despite his detestation of the ancient traditions of his country, Peter I was thoroughly a Russian. Moreover, even if some of his actions horrified his own people just as much as they shocked the West, he typified the characteristics of the Russians—innate shrewdness, endurance, contempt for luxury, tenacity.

Peter, however, went further than his countrymen. He was not only the greatest monarch in Russian history, but his knowledge and vision made him one of the foremost figures of his day.

Weighing against the less favorable aspects of his character was the fact that although he built an empire, he was never corrupted by power. His personal retinue, which included nobles and commoners, numbered no more than a dozen.

It seems odd, perhaps, that truth and justice meant so much to a man who could sanction dreadful torture and resort to murder. Yet he was anxious to impose law and order on his people. He wanted them to have a strong sense of loyalty to the state. This he made apparent, especially near the end of his reign, in his approach to those responsible for administration. Appealing for honesty, he stressed that the slightest straying from the truth was akin to treason.

In his campaign to rid the nation of idleness, Peter presented himself as an example, especially in time of war. In 1713, Admiral Cruys pleaded with him not to run personal risks in a naval battle. Peter replied: "It is eighteen years now since I began to serve my country and no one yet has asked me to stay at home like a small child. To take one's pay and not do one's service would be shameful."

It was also characteristic—and unusual for one in his capacity—that he did not assume high military rank at the outset. As Captain John Perry, the English engineer in his employ, pointed out, Peter did not take the rank of pilot until the campaign at Azov.

At the time of the Great Embassy he started out as a sergeant of the Guard and later assumed the rank of captain. It was eight more years before he took the rank of colonel. And not until after the battle at Poltava did he take the rank of lieutenant general. Usually, however, he did not personally lead his troops into battle, but drew up the operational plans, and traveled about Russia, organizing the munitions factories and the shipbuilding operations.

Peter accepted payment for his services. This was often received at a function, such as a banquet, and Romodanovsky would thank him for devoting himself to Russia. This may appear a trifle ridiculous, but at least it demonstrated that the Tsar did not expect of others what he was not prepared to do himself.

This amazing autocrat, who was not very intellectual, found happiness in personal industry. It is well known that he was skilled in government, diplomacy, and the strategy of war, but he was also adept in other spheres. With justification Peter could claim to be a carpenter, engineer, gunner, artificer, armorer, ironsmith, dentist, and cabinetmaker. It was also said that he was competent as a surgeon and once operated on a foreign merchant suffering from dropsy.

These skills bear eloquent witness to Peter's widespread interests, especially in practical matters. As an innovator, he was responsible for the first hospital in Moscow. Through Peter, Russia received the telescope and a translation of a book on astronomy. Among other things he tried to foster an interest in geography. At his request Evreinov and Luzhin, two of Russia's pioneer cartographers, journeyed to the Far East. Their instructions were to travel as far as latitude 75 degrees to ascertain if America and Asia were joined together. Also, they were to report on the Kurile Islands, which had been discovered by Cossacks.

Peter had a profound curiosity which infected others. In the closing years of his reign he launched an attempt to piece together a picture of Arctic Siberia. Work began in 1725, the year of his death, but seventeen years were to elapse before the project was completed. Paramount in these plans was the Great Northern Expedition which, among other things, sought to locate a passage to China and India through the Arctic. Tsar Peter had ordered the construction of vessels sturdy enough to resist the ice along the northern coast of Siberia and to allow the charting of the East Siberian and Chukchi seas.

He put Captain Vitus Bering, a Danish naval officer who had served the Russian navy for twenty years, in charge of the expedition. Spanberg, also a Dane, and Chirikov, a Russian, were Bering's assistants. Ahead lay incredible hardships. Two ships were built at Okhotsk, and in July, 1728, Bering discovered the strait between Asia and America that now bears his name.

The significance of all this is that Russians in the eighteenth century, inspired in the first place by Peter, went on to probe much more of the Arctic. The work has continued, so that Russia today can rightly claim to have made far more progress in the north than any other nation. Peter sent men into Siberia and they discovered many minerals. The value of the early exploration is shown by the rich mineral deposits that are now being worked in that region.

Despite all his practical activity, Peter did not neglect matters of state. He often began work at five in the morning. According to an intimate, the Tsar "penetrates and understands them [state affairs] better than anyone of his ministers; he is present at all their deliberations."

No aspect of Russian life was too insignificant to

receive his attention. His decrees dealt with such contrasting subjects as the reduction of taxes on bathing establishments and the preservation of the forests. Apart from the decrees, there were orders in letters, which reveal his temperament.

The Tsar was notoriously moody, changing abruptly from a gay mood to a melancholy one, and becoming a man impossible to deal with.

Sometimes his mood was expressed in his mockery of the Orthodox Church through the Prince-Pope and his "cardinals." But it should not be concluded from this that Peter lacked piety. On the contrary, he not only believed in God but thought that he himself was ruled by the divine will. When fighting the Muslims, he regarded himself as the champion of Christendom. And throughout his campaigns he always thanked God for victory.

It had been traditional for Peter's predecessors to participate in religious services. This was one custom which Peter did not wish to abolish. He sang the canticles from memory, and was always ready to take his place in the choir. In Europe, theologians were amazed, during conversations with Peter, to discover the depth of his religious knowledge. Many of his letters concluded with the words, "God's will be done."

13

ALEXIS THE REACTIONARY

Even though he believed in God, Peter did not allow the Church to impede the progress of the state. He worshiped his country. Indeed, one can say that he dedicated his life to the state with the result that he neglected his family. This led to complex and tragic situations.

Peter's neglect most noticeably affected his son Alexis, who was partly the victim of the conflicting personalities of his parents. Eudoxia was conservative and clung to the past. Peter loathed tradition and was bent on reform. By traveling in Russia and abroad, and also spending considerable time on his military campaigns, Peter saw little of his son in the boy's early years.

Consequently, Alexis—utterly unlike his father both in temperament and ability—came under the influence of Eudoxia and her ideas. After his mother was banished to a convent, Alexis was entrusted to the care of Natalia, Peter's sister. Two Germans became his tutors. Peter wished to interest his son in Western ideas, and at one period intended to have his education completed in Europe. The plan, however, never materialized. Instead, when the tutors left Moscow for diplomatic reasons, Alexis was left to his own resources and to the pressures of people who hated his father's reforms.

It was not surprising that by the time Alexis was fifteen years old, he disliked the activities of his father. The son has been described as weak in character and indolent, and there is much to support this accusation. To avoid fulfilling duties, Alexis sometimes made himself ill by drinking medicines and he also invented ridiculous excuses. He once even resorted to the extreme measure of shooting himself in the hand.

Even so, had Alexis had normal parents and a stable childhood he might have developed finer qualities. His boyhood setting was the din and commotion of Preobrazhenskoye and the noisy roistering and drinking, as well as the tortures and the executions. Over all was the towering figure of Peter and his moments of terrible rage.

With a disposition that differed so sharply from his father's, it is understandable that Alexis sought escape in drink and in the companionship of the discontented. Unlike his father, Alexis was drawn to things that were essentially Russian. Therefore, many prayed for the day when he would ascend the throne, believing that he would banish all aliens and revert to former customs.

Alexis bore some physical resemblance to his father. But there the likeness ended. Although tall, the boy was of delicate physique and lacked the vigor or will to continue the policies of his father. On the other hand, he was not without talent. Whereas Peter was of a practical nature, Alexis was essentially the intellectual. An avid reader, his favorite books were the Bible, and those dealing with the lives of the saints and Byzantine lore. He was particularly drawn to theological dogma.

Some idea of the disparity between father and son was demonstrated by Alexis' visit to Germany in 1709. The reason for the visit was to study geometry and fortifications, but he preferred to delve into the history of the Middle Ages.

Apparently, Alexis admired his father but he feared him, too. Most probably the young man developed a complex once he realized that he could never rise to such greatness. He must have been aware, too, of his lack of will to enforce reform. There seems no evidence that Alexis was at first disloyal to his father. It is simply that he was so different from the Tsar.

With the rank of Sergeant of the Guard, Alexis traveled with Peter to some of the battlefronts. At eighteen years of age, he was made governor of Moscow. Although lacking a taste for war, he recruited troops for his father, organized food supplies for the army, arranged for collection of taxes, and was in charge of fortifications. Thus, in the capacity of quartermaster general Alexis was valuable to Peter. Alexis was also responsible for the festivities in Moscow after the victory at Poltava. The acclaim with which Muscovites hailed him was proof of his popularity. To them he represented at least one member of the house of Romanov who would fulfill all that was expected of a tsar. In 1711, Alexis gleaned some idea of what it would be like to be the head of state. While Peter was fighting the Prut campaign, Alexis was elevated to the regency in his absence. Unfortunately, he could not muster enthusiasm for war, administration, or Western ways.

Perhaps Peter decided that the surest way to Westernize his son, and to prepare him as successor, was to marry him to a German princess. The intended bride was Princess Charlotte of Brunswick. While studying in Dresden in 1709, Alexis visited Charlotte at the castle of Wolfenbüttel. He had not received his father's proposal with enthusiasm but had submitted to Peter's wishes. The Tsar had doubtless looked at the marriage not in the interests of his son, but purely as a means to Westernize him. Peter realized that most Russians would have preferred a Russian bride for the young heir; a Russian marriage for the young prince would better their chances to revert to the old system. There can be little doubt that Peter was conscious of this. It seemed obvious that unless Alexis changed his attitude, all reforms would cease once the son had succeeded. A marriage to a German, however, might Westernize the Russian court to some degree. For instance, a male offspring would be half German, would receive a German education, and would have many German relatives.

The Tsar was preparing for his Balkan campaign when the marriage deed was brought from Wolfenbüttel to Yarovov. After his defeat on the Prut in 1711, Peter traveled to Carlsbad for two reasons: to bathe in the waters in the hope of improving his health and to arrange the marriage of Alexis and Charlotte. But he grew so ill during part of the journey that he was removed from the coach and borne on a stretcher. When Peter became well again toward the end of September, he decided that the wedding should be solemnized at Torgau on the Elbe River, where the couple was already living with the queen of Poland.

Alexis still showed no enthusiasm for the union, and Father Jacob Ignatief, his confessor, was aware of this. The Church had advised the young prince to be evasive, but Alexis was too weak to resist his father's will.

Indeed, Alexis' attitude toward his marriage mirrors his weak nature. Peter had earlier placed him in an embarrassing situation. Before the marriage had been finally agreed upon, Charlotte's relatives had insisted that Peter should pay the bride an endowment of twenty-five thousand rubles and a sum of fifty thousand rubles each year. On his father's instructions, Alexis attempted but failed to persuade Charlotte's family to agree to reduce the annuity by ten thousand rubles. The family insisted further that the money should be paid even in the event of Alexis' death. Somewhat resignedly the young man had written to Peter: "I have tried very hard to get them to ask less."

The bride was related to Augustus, King of Poland, who had succeeded in getting money from the Tsar. Possibly Charlotte and her family, who had probably agreed to the alliance because of its financial value, decided to do likewise. In any event, a number of the less affluent members of the German aristocracy took the marriage as the opportunity to live at the expense of the house of Romanov.

On November 14, 1711, Alexis and Charlotte were married. After three days of festivities the bridegroom was dispatched by Peter to Thorn to provision the army then besieging Stralsund. Charlotte was reunited with Alexis on December 19, and she remained with him for four months.

Although Peter and Catherine had been secretly married in Petersburg in 1707, they were publicly wed in Menshikov's private chapel in Moscow in February, 1712. But many in Russia still regarded Eudoxia as the legal Tsaritsa. Peter knew this, and because of the particular circumstances of his union with Catherine, it has been suggested that he was jealous of his son and his "legal" marriage.

Whatever the cause, Peter became increasingly hostile to Alexis. After the marriage, Peter referred to his son as the Crown Prince (in the German manner) and not as Tsarevitch, his traditional title. Charlotte was the Crown Princess. But Alexis was given nothing more than a soldier's pay and Charlotte's annuity was withheld. Visiting the couple at Thorn, Menshikov was astonished by the manner in which Alexis and his wife were compelled to live, and he felt obliged to lend Charlotte five thousand rubles.

Menshikov told Alexis that, on the Tsar's orders, he was to join the army in Pomerania. Again separated from her husband, Charlotte went to Elbing to wait for him and for the annuity from the Tsar. By October, 1712, Alexis and Charlotte were still apart. Why Peter allowed this situation to persist is not clear. It is known, however, that he asked Charlotte to journey to Russia. "As soon as money comes I shall carry out the command of your Imperial Majesty," she replied.

Instead of sending money, the Tsar instructed Alexis to return to Russia and take Charlotte with him. But when Alexis reached Elbing in December, he found that Charlotte had gone back to her family in Brunswick.

So far as Charlotte was concerned, her action had the desired effect. In the following months Peter sent her fifteen thousand rubles in cash and a draft for a large sum. During February, 1713, while traveling in the area, Peter called at Brunswick. Charlotte agreed to rejoin Alexis in Russia, but by the time she reached

Petersburg in May, Alexis had left with the Tsar for Finland.

When Alexis returned to Petersburg, he was cold and indifferent to his wife, and spent much time drinking with his companions. Cronies flattered him, explaining how many people in Russia looked to him to return the nation to the old Muscovite ways upon Peter's death.

Assessing all the factors, it appears that the tragedy of Alexis was that, whether he wished it or not, as heir to the throne he was thought of by the people as the one to lead them. But he was too weak in character, and in any event had no desire to head a revolt. He was guilty of indiscretions against Peter in moments of drunkenness, but he quickly rejected them when he was sober.

Peter was aware that his enemies might use Alexis as a pawn in a plot to destroy all that had been accomplished. "My father," he said, "had to fight a single beard, the Patriarch; I have thousands against me."

This was no exaggeration. Peter was hated by many in all sections of society. He roused deep antagonism because of his attitude toward the Church and toward traditions, and for his persistence in waging wars that were thought to be futile and unnecessary. Husbands and sons were taken away, many of them never to return. The people were bewildered. He had "knouted" the nation into accepting many things which they could not properly understand. In short, the people accused him of strange antics; he was attacked for having drained happiness from national life.

Many of the nobles were just as hostile, condemning the Tsar for promoting to power men of low birth, such as Menshikov. They resented the severity of his decrees, which aimed to cleanse the country of what Peter referred to as idle gentry. To the nobles it was inconceivable that they should be forced to register for military service. Punishment for absenteeism was even worse: anyone who exposed an absentee had the right to receive his estate. Later, an absentee ran the risk of death. Thus, Peter, uncouth and harsh, knew that during his many illnesses a large number of his subjects were anxious for his death. He was civilizing his people, but they preferred the Russia of the past—and so did his son.

14

MONK OR HEIR?

In the spring of 1714, Alexis became ill. On his doctors' advice he journeyed to Carlsbad for treatment during mid-June, although Charlotte was due to deliver her child in a month. Peter declared that Charlotte would receive the best medical attention, but if he was hoping for a grandson he was disappointed. On July 12, a girl was born. She was christened Natalia after the Tsar's mother.

Alexis appears to have been totally indifferent to his child. He communicated with no one in Russia before he finally returned there in December. Soon he was seeking refuge in drunkenness and the companionship of a Finnish girl named Afrosinia.

For some time Peter had held little regard for his son, but at this period his contempt must have been considerable. In his heir he saw a weakling dominated by drink and debauchery. What future could there be for Russia if the monarchy were entrusted to such a man? But there was no other male to continue the dynasty.

One thing was certain: with Alexis on the throne, the dissidents would quickly gain control and sweep away Peter's reforms. In his drunken bouts Alexis had made unwise remarks against the Tsar. On Peter's death he would get rid of his father's intimates. He would live not in Petersburg but in Moscow. He would not keep up the ships, and he would merely maintain an army that was big enough for defense.

It is probable that through his informers Peter was aware of his son's remarks. Yet for the time being he took no action—not until 1715, when the family drama reached its peak. On October 22, Charlotte gave birth to a son; then Catherine gave birth to a son on November 3. The subsequent alarm of the Tsarevitch was not groundless. Rumor had reached him that, in the event Catherine bore a male heir, Peter planned to disinherit his first son.

In order to do that, the Tsar would have to secure evidence to convince the nation that Alexis was unfit to succeed; without this proof Peter knew that, on his death, Alexis would establish his claim to the throne.

Charlotte died shortly after the birth of her child, and

Alexis received a letter of reproach from the Tsar on the day of the funeral. It was dated eleven days before the birth of Charlotte's son. There is a theory that Peter delayed sending the letter, waiting to see if Charlotte's child would be a boy. What is a fact is that Peter now openly denounced his first son.

After describing how Russia had prevailed against Swedish oppression, the Tsar wrote: "But when considering this joy given to the Fatherland by God I think of the line of succession, my joy is almost entirely eaten up, seeing thee, the heir, wholly incapable of managing State affairs (for God is not to blame, for He did not deprive thee of reason, nor did He entirely withhold from thee physical strength: for although thou art not very strong thou art not altogether weak); and moreover thou dost not wish to hear of military affairs or of how we went from darkness to light and those who did not know us in the darkness now respect us. I do not teach that one should be willing to make war without lawful reason, but that one should love war and do all that is possible to instruct and equip oneself; for that is one of the two indispensable things in Government, that disorders be quelled and the country defended.

"If," Peter went on, "you object that generals do not depend on a will above them, that certainly is no excuse, for each looks to the head in order to follow his wishes, which is obvious, for in the days of the rule of my brother did not everyone love costumes and horses?

But now arms; although there are those to whom neither the one nor the other mean anything; but to whatever one shows an inclination all will show inclination and from what one turns away all will turn away. And if men turn quickly away from light amusements, how much more from the serious ones (namely, guns). Moreover, as you have no inclination, you learn nothing, and so do not know military affairs.

"And what if thou dost not know how to govern nor how to reward the good and punish the neglectful, not understanding the forces at work? Thou wouldst have to look into somebody else's mouth like a young bird. Dost thou excuse thy liability to take part in military affairs? But that is not a reason, for it is not work but will that I wish, and that is dependent upon no disease. Ask any who remember my aforementioned brother, who was much more sickly than thou and could not even ride on a mettlesome horse but was so much interested that he was a constant spectator and kept a better stable than exists now. Thou seest—that it is not great labors, but will that matters. . . .

"Considering all these matters, I turn again to the first, discussing thyself, for as I am a human being and subject to death, to whom then shall I leave the plantation which with the help of the Highest I have somewhat tended? What merits the idle slave of the Gospel who buried his talent in the earth (that is, flung away all that God had given him)? Add to that I recall the evil and obstinate morals that possess thee! How often have

I scolded thee for all that, and not only scolded but flogged, and think how many years I have not spoken to thee; but nothing has succeeded, nothing has helped, all has been gratuitous, all to one side, and thou dost not wish to do anything, only to live at home and make merry, and in the latter matter repulsively.

"However, all is for the best! The madman rejoices in his misfortune, not grasping what may result from it (St. Paul writes the truth: how can that one rule the Church of God who is neglectful in his own house?) not only to thee, but to the whole State. Thinking upon all this with affliction, and seeing that nothing I can do inclines thee to good, I have for the common welfare determined to write thee this last testament, and wait a little in case thou shouldst now behave without hypocrisy.

"But if not, then be it known that I will wholly cut thee off from the succession, like a gangrenous limb, and do not say to thyself that thou art the only son I have and this is only written to frighten: Verily (God willing) I will carry it out, for my Fatherland and my people I have not spared and do not spare my life, how therefore should I spare thee, a worthless one? Will not a good stranger be better than my own worthless?"

This letter conveys to a great extent Peter's attitude to the state and to life in general. It is clear that he was anxious about the future of Russia. The letter also illustrates the striking difference in character between father and son. Peter was strong and ambitious for the good of his country. Alexis was weak and utterly without ambition either for himself or for Russia. He sought nothing more than to retire from public and military life.

But could Peter be satisfied with Alexis' retirement and nothing more? As long as Alexis lived, he would be the figure around whom all the discontented would rally. The Tsarevitch was the lawful heir and, unlike Peter, he was popular with the Russian people. No matter what the Tsar decreed, it could be reversed by popular opinion after his death, if Alexis lived.

Did Peter word his letter in order to frighten Alexis, or was he trying to create a situation in which he could destroy him? Peter loved his country; perhaps he was even willing to sacrifice his son for it.

The reply which the Tsar received from Alexis was somewhat baffling in its simplicity. Agreeing that he should be disinherited, Alexis wrote a few days after receiving his father's letter: "Most gracious sovereign father! On the 27th of October, 1715, day of the funeral of my wife, I read what was sent me from thee, and I will have no more to say except that if it be thy will to deprive me of the succession to the Russian Crown, then be it according to thy will. Concerning which, sir, I most humbly pray you: that since I am useless and worthless for this business and also quite lacking in memory (without which it is not possible to do anything), and since as a result of various illnesses all my intellectual and physical forces have been weakened and I have become worthless for the government of such a great people which needs a man not so rotten as I, for the sake of that, for the succession (God give you many years of health) of Russia after you (though I had no brother, now, thank God, I have a brother whom God grant health). I do not pretend, and in the future will not pretend, as God is my witness, and for clear evidence I write it with my own hand. I entrust my children to your will and ask for myself subsistence till death. Placing all these matters at the disposal of your judgment and gracious will, your most submissive slave and son, Alexis."

At this time the Tsar's illness worsened, and doctors thought he was about to die. He was given the sacraments, but Alexander Kikin, a noble who hated Peter's regime, counseled Alexis to be wary. Kikin claimed that the Tsar merely feigned serious illness to discover how Alexis and his followers would respond.

On January 19, 1716, the Tsar again wrote to his son. He was still not convinced that Alexis would keep his word: ". . . I now answer that I have read thy letter to my first letter; in it thou art only concerned with the succession and thou placest at the disposal of my will what always was there without thy words. But why dost thou not make express answer to my letter, for I wrote much more about deficiency of will and lack of interest in affairs than about the physical weakness about which alone thou repliest? And although it was severely written thou takest no notice of the fact that for several years I have been displeased with thee.

"For that reason I consider that thou dost not pay a very great deal of attention to thy father's warning, which prompts me to write these further words; for now that thou fearest nothing how wilt thou keep a covenant with me? As for the oath thou takest, I cannot, in my aforementioned severity of mood, believe it. As David said: all men are liars. Although thou mightest sincerely wish to keep that oath, thou mightest well be inclined and forced to break it by the long-beards who, thanks to thy parasitism, are encouraged to no advantage and to whom thou art mightily sympathetic.

"I ask again, in what way does thy birth honor thy father? Dost thou, having quite grown up, help me in my insupportable griefs and labors? Not a wit. Everyone knows thou rather hatest my doings on behalf of my people, accomplished not sparing my own health and of which absolutely thou wilt be the destroyer. For that reason it is impossible for thee to remain as thou wishest, neither meat nor fish; either change thy habits and become sincerely worthy of the inheritance, or be a monk: for without this being settled my spirit cannot be at rest, especially just now that my health is so poor. To this, upon receipt, reply without delay, either by letter or to me personally, stating thy resolve. But if thou dost not, then I shall deal with thee as with an evil-doer. Peter."

The Tsarevitch was wholeheartedly in favor of entering the Church, and he agreed to become a monk. As Kikin and Prince Viasemsky, his childhood guardian, pointed out: "The cowl is not nailed to the head; it can be taken off again." And so on the following day the prince replied: ". . . I received your letter, but cannot answer it at greater length on account of my illness. I desire monastic rank and for that ask your gracious permission. Your slave and unworthy son. Alexis."

In spite of this letter, the Tsar was still undecided about what to do. But at that time the Northern War temporarily ousted the dynastic succession from Peter's mind. With relief, Alexis and his friends heard that the Tsar was to leave for Denmark.

15

JUDICIAL MURDER

Did absence soften Peter's attitude toward his son? On August 26, 1716, the Tsar, who was now forty-four years old, again wrote to Alexis, asking him to think seriously about monastic life. Alexis could now enter the Church or join Peter in Copenhagen, "for thou still hast time to get here for action."

Monastic life did appeal to the Tsarevitch, but Afrosinia, the woman he had been seeing since shortly after his marriage, held greater attraction for him. He wished to marry her. Leaving Moscow, he traveled to Petersburg where he assured Menshikov that he would journey to Denmark. But either his nerve failed him or his action was premeditated, for he played truant. Adopting the name of Kokhansky, he fled with Afrosinia to the court of Vienna to seek the protection of the Austrian emperor, who was his brother-in-law.

During November, 1716, in an emotional state, Alexis informed the vice-chancellor that the Tsar wished to deprive him of his life and the succession of his children to the throne. He attributed his own weakness of character to Menshikov who, years earlier, had upset his health by drunkenness. The Tsar, Alexis explained, had been kind to him until the birth of the children, his own and the Tsar's by Catherine.

"She and Prince Menshikov constantly set my father against me," Alexis said. "Both are evil people, godless, and conscienceless. I am in no way guilty of wrong to my father. . . . The Tsaritsa and Menshikov wish to kill me or hide me away in a monastery. I have never wished to be a soldier, but some years ago my father gave me administrative work to do and all went well; my father was pleased. But when my children were born, my wife died, and the Tsaritsa bore a son, they wished to torture me to death or drive me to death by drink. . . . I heard that the partisans of Menshikov and the Tsaritsa, apprehensive of my father's health, wished to poison me. That is why I pretended to journey to my father. . . ."

The Austrian Emperor Charles VI gave Alexis and Afrosinia sanctuary at Erenburg Castle in the Tyrol. This became known to Veselovsky, the Russian minister at Vienna, who informed Captain Rumiantsef of the

Guard and three fellow officers, whom Peter ordered to capture the prince.

Peter's agents, however, were unsuccessful. So, too, were official representations made to the emperor who, on May 6, 1717, had the Tsarevitch and his companion disguised and conveyed under guard to the fortress of St. Elmo in Naples. Because the emperor was also the king of Naples, Alexis still came under his protection.

Now began tedious diplomatic exchanges during which the aged Peter Tolstoy entered the scene. Two months elapsed before Tolstoy and Rumiantsef persuaded the Austrian ruler to let them visit the prince.

On September 26, Tolstoy and Rumiantsef delivered to Alexis a letter from Peter, accusing the son of having placed himself, like a traitor, under foreign protection. Alexis had brought grief and shame to himself and the fatherland. "If thou art still in fear of me," wrote Peter, "then I assure thee, and promise by God and his judgment, that there will be no punishment of thee, but if thou wilt obey me and return I will show thee my best love. But if thou wilt not obey, then as father, with the power given me by God, I curse thee eternally, and as thy sovereign I denounce thee as a traitor, and I shall leave no means untried to bring thee to justice as a traitor and abuser of thy father. Yet remember I did not always use force with thee, and once wished to leave everything to thy will. . . ."

Alexis declined to give an answer at once, and two days later, despite the threatening attitude of the Tsar's two emissaries, he was still evasive. The Tsarevitch knew that promises were sometimes broken by his father.

The emperor evidently did not understand the situation. Imagining that Afrosinia was the cause of the dispute, he threatened to take her away. Tolstoy lied to Alexis, telling him that Peter was already leading an army to take him prisoner. Bribed by Tolstoy, the secretary of the Viceroy of Naples informed Alexis that the emperor's protection would cease once Peter's pardon ended. Finally the Tsarevitch yielded.

Tolstoy agreed to the prince's request that he marry Afrosinia and live quietly in the country in Russia. The Tsar also wrote confirming these terms.

Thus, the party left Naples. One can imagine the nervous tension as Alexis drew near to the Russian frontier. Afrosinia, who was going to have a child, was left at the Russian port of Riga on the Baltic Sea, but the prince was forced to proceed to Petersburg, arriving there early in 1718.

The Tsar's treatment of his son from that time on exposes some of Peter's strange and worst qualities. He was notorious for the way he changed his mind, even dishonoring promises. He altered his views to satisfy his prevailing whims and moods. Perhaps he thought that this was the prerogative of the Tsar. Possibly when he wrote to his son in Naples, it was a deliberate act of treachery. But there is nothing to prove this. Yet after having assured Alexis of his pardon, the Tsar's subsequent behavior was a dark stain on his character; it was despicable and detracted considerably from his greatness.

Maybe Alexis had spoken the truth when he had charged that Menshikov and Catherine wished to destroy him. Although there is no evidence, perhaps these two dominant personalities did induce the Tsar to revoke his pardon. Both would have had reasons for doing so. Catherine wished to see her son, Peter Petrovich, as the Tsar's successor. But if Alexis sat on the throne, his own son, Peter Alexeevich, would be the lawful heir. As for Menshikov, he knew that Kikin and others would quickly end his power should Alexis inherit the crown.

On February 3, 1718, Alexis was brought before his father and a gathering of prominent priests and laymen in the Kremlin palace. Denounced by the Tsar, the prince again begged forgiveness. This was promised on two conditions: that he renounce the crown in favor of his stepbrother, and that he expose those on whose advice he had fled to Austria. Alexis complied with both requests, and the Tsar issued a public manifesto recalling the old accusations against his son, whom, he claimed, should have been punished by death.

Peter browbeat the nation, declaring that all who accepted Alexis as his heir would be treated as traitors. This was no idle threat. A clerk named Dokukin, who loyally supported the prince, refused to accept the compulsory renunciation of the succession. Beneath the formal oath he wrote: ". . . I shall not kiss the life-giving Cross of Christ; nor will I sign this with my hand. I offer with this a small extract from a book of divinity by Nazianzin, which amply justifies my action. . . ."

This was the genuine belief of a man who was willing to suffer for the truth. He personally handed the form to the Tsar. One might have thought that such honesty and courage would have appealed to Peter. But in a situation such as this there was nothing noble in the Tsar's nature. Peter knew that he was not popular with the people, and that Alexis was. Any leniency might have been interpreted as a sign of weakness and an incentive to others to express their resentment more forcefully. The fate of Dokukin was a terrible one. Tortured on three occasions, he was finally broken on the wheel. (It is rather strange that, as the object of so much hatred, attempts were not made to assassinate the Tsar. But no such incident ever occurred, although the chances to destroy him were frequent, for Peter moved freely without a guard.)

When Peter asked for the details of his son's flight to Vienna, Alexis was threatened with the loss of his pardon if he withheld even the slightest bit of information. Because of this, Kikin was caught, tortured, and subjected to a ghastly death. One collaborator was beheaded, another banished to Archangel, and another to Siberia. The police interrogated many, and Eudoxia's life was also endangered. On the Tsar's orders, on February 4, an army officer went to the convent of

Suzdal where Eudoxia had taken her vows twenty years earlier, and brought her back to Moscow.

In a letter to the Tsar, Eudoxia, now forty-five years old, confessed that after a year she ceased to be a nun but stayed on quietly at the convent as a lay person in disguise. "My secret has been revealed by Gregory Pisarev. Now I rely on the humane generosity of your Majesty. . . . I beg mercy for my crime . . . that I may not die a useless death." She begged to return to the life of a nun.

Under torture, nuns at the convent admitted that there was an illicit relationship between Eudoxia and a recruiting officer named Stephen Glebov. There were more lashes of the knout. Indeed, it is said that this beating of women—even young girls—grew more commonplace in Peter's later years.

Courageously, Glebov, although tortured and finally impaled, refused to involve others, but spat contemptuously in the face of the Tsar. Yet Peter finally learned the truth from his own son, and the evidence incriminated Bishop Dosithei at Rostov. He, too, was defiant, admitting that he had had a vision at the convent and had prophesied that Eudoxia would again share the throne.

Unfrocked in public, Dosithei fearlessly called on fellow bishops to go to the people. "What is in everyone's heart today?" he cried. When tortured, the bishop confessed that he wanted the Tsar to die and be replaced by Alexis. For his truthfulness, after the usual agonies on the wheel, Dosithei was mutilated and his head exhibited on the end of a pole.

There were more decapitations. Eudoxia was allowed to live, but was subject to rigid discipline at an island convent on Lake Ladoga.

If it is true that Alexis never attempted to speak for his mother or anyone else—and there is nothing on record to indicate that he did—the whole affair indicates his weakness of character. And if he thought that the executions sealed his safety, he was mistaken.

Finally the prince returned to Petersburg with the Tsar, eagerly awaiting Afrosinia. But there was to be no happy reunion. She reached Petersburg in mid-April, to be imprisoned at once in the local fortress.

Fear of torture induced her to betray her prince. At first glance, the willingness with which she talked seems contemptible, until one considers the terror which the Tsar could inspire. On April 20, he questioned her himself. She revealed how Alexis had denounced the Tsar to the Austrian emperor, and how he had written to bishops promising a return to old traditions after Peter's death. On one occasion, she said, Alexis had been happy to learn of the illness of Catherine's son, and elated by the news of an army mutiny.

In some measure all this was already known to the Tsar. Thus, despite his smoldering anger, Peter released Afrosinia, and Alexis still remained free. However, in the following weeks, it is generally believed that Alexis was flogged and questioned. In any event, on June 14, 1718, he was thrown in jail.

Perhaps wishing to clear his conscience, the Tsar had already requested Church leaders to issue a signed authorization as to the form of punishment. Yavorsky and other ecclesiastics were somewhat noncommittal, informing Peter that Holy Writ offered similar instances should he decide to pardon his son.

Clearly Peter did not find this to his liking. He now ordered that the crown prince be brought before the Senate on June 19. Tolstoy presided. More beatings brought the confession from Alexis that he had hoped for the Tsar's death. His father confessor had assured him of God's forgiveness—"for we all wish it." When tortured, the confessor corroborated the prince's words.

On June 22, Peter instructed Tolstoy to question Alexis on three points. Why had he not obeyed his father? Why was he not afraid of punishment? Why did he wish to keep the succession by a method other than obedience? Whatever took place in the fortress, Alexis was doomed by the answers that Tolstoy conveyed to the Tsar. Alexis had undergone a ferocious lashing three days earlier, and on the morning of June 24—the day after Peter received Tolstoy's report—the Tsarevitch was again flogged with the knout. Later that day the special commission that scrutinized the evidence recommended a sentence of death. It was announced that Alexis had sacrificed his pardon by concealing details of a plot to murder the Tsar. To Tolstoy, the prince was said to have revealed that he "was not willing to await the death of his father and sovereign to receive the succession to the throne, but was ready with the aid of mutineers to take it by force, and not only that, but he placed his reliance on foreign aid and armed intervention. . . . In that way the Tsarevitch has shown himself wholly undeserving of that mercy and forgiveness which his father and sovereign had promised him."

Alexis was not executed in public. He died in the fortress on June 26, but there is little to describe precisely how. With the Tsar, Menshikov, and Tolstoy among them, a group of people visited the prince's cell about eight o'clock in the morning, bringing with them instruments of torture. The official account explains that the "rack was applied at eleven o'clock. Then they dispersed. That same day, at six o'clock in the afternoon, the Tsarevitch gave up his soul."

The crown prince had been judicially murdered.

16

"FATHER OF HIS PEOPLE"

Alexis is described as the first political prisoner to be incarcerated in the fortress at Petersburg. The Tsar circulated a report among the courts of Europe that the prince had succumbed to apoplexy on hearing the death sentence. But could one accept his word? Archives testify that Alexis was tortured on his final morning. Was this intended to end his life?

Various rumors attempt to describe the prince's death. One relates how, because his life still lingered, Catherine commissioned a surgeon to sever the arteries. This is how the Dutch ambassador explained the death to his government. A report received by the Austrian emperor, however, attributed death to beheading.

Exactly how Alexis died remains a mystery to this day. For all we know, Peter himself might have been the executioner.

What is historical truth is that in the next few days the Tsar, in high spirits, attended two celebrations: to observe the anniversary of Poltava and for the launching of a ninety-four-gun vessel. There were the usual feastings and fireworks while the dead prince lay in the cathedral. It seems incongruous that Catherine and the Tsar should, like many Muscovites, kiss the young man's face when paying their final tribute.

Because of the prince's crime, no mourning was worn by the court. Alexis was buried beside Charlotte. Afrosinia, the woman he had loved, received an ample portion of his estate. Then, with her child, she vanished from the scene.

The Tsar's major reforms had been accomplished. Indeed, had he himself died in that year he would have already done enough to change Russia drastically. His chief concern now was to ensure that the nation would not abandon those reforms after his death. In these last years he remarked that his present occupations were a game compared with his labors to build an army and a fleet. "I had to teach my people not only science," he said, "but also courage and fidelity, and that did not go easily. I thank God from the bottom of my heart that He has granted me this leisure. . . ."

Peter could now devote more time to Petersburg and its society. He had broken down the old Muscovite hostility and apathy to foreign elements. The citizens of his new capital formed a mixed society, Russians and aliens intermingled. Moreover, it was no longer a society in which males were predominant. The Tsar had emancipated Russian women. Never in the whole of the nation's history had they known such freedom. More liberalism, unfortunately, led to more immorality in which Peter himself set the example.

One of Peter's innovations were the "assemblies," and he even introduced a measure compelling people to attend them. These assemblies were somewhat like modern social clubs and grew quite popular. From 1718, they were held three times weekly, first in public halls and then in big private houses. When possible, rooms were set apart for games, discussion, and dancing which, with chess, were the Tsar's favorite pastimes. Wine broke down any Russian reserve. Anyone who caused displeasure was punished by having to drink a huge goblet—the Cup of the Great Eagle—filled with wine or brandy.

Drinking was forced on society whether it wanted it or not. Because of recurring ill-health, the Tsar now at times accepted his doctors' advice and drank less. But he derived satisfaction in making others drink to excess. He even locked the doors to prevent his guests from escaping. The orgies, which had characterized life at Preobrazhenskoye, were also held in Petersburg. So were the fantastic rites of the Prince-Pope.

There were not only festive moments but also

moments of sadness, such as the mourning of the dead. Peter would sometimes lead the funeral processions of both the illustrious and more ordinary people. But even at times of death there was an element of burlesque. When, for instance, the chef of the imperial kitchens died, the body was accompanied by hundreds of men from the Guards dressed as master cooks.

The Northern War still dragged on even when Charles XII was killed in November, 1718. But it had lost a good deal of its severity. The peace which the Tsar so keenly sought proved elusive, partly because of the intrigues of George I of England. Yet when Russian forces invaded the Swedish coast in 1719, and during the following year, there could be little doubt as to the final outcome.

After the signing of the Treaty of Nystad, Peter sailed from Petersburg in his Prussian yacht and on September 3, 1721, in the Gulf of Finland, met the couriers bringing the document. The next day, at Petersburg, he stood ecstatically on the deck shouting "Peace! Peace!" to the excited crowds in the harbor. From a platform already erected in the Square of the Trinity, Peter cried: "Hail, Orthodox people! And thank Almighty God, who has terminated this long war which lasted twenty-one years, and has given us eternal happy peace with Sweden!"

Jubilation was expressed in a cacophony of church bells, and thunderous cannon and carbines. Trumpets blared and the air crackled and blasted with fireworks.

Beer was free and plentiful and drunkenness was rife. On September 10, there began a court masquerade which continued for a week. A thousand revelers met daily in different parts of Petersburg, covering their gay dresses with dark cloaks when they visited the cathedral.

The festivities went on throughout Russia for weeks—a national occasion during which the people temporarily forgot the Tsar's reforms and shared in his victory. For Peter, now forty-nine years old, the celebrations culminated in more glory on October 20. The Senate rewarded him with the title of Emperor and designated him "the Great." He would be known, too, as "the Father of His People."

In the fortress there was particular rejoicing, for in the morning a general pardon was announced for the condemned. Peter had described it as "moldy" when the Senate suggested that he should be known as Emperor of the East. He preferred the title "All-Russian Emperor." In the cathedral two days later Prokopovich eulogized the sovereign's life. After receiving the salutations of Chancellor Golovin and a number of senators, Peter, addressing the congregation, attributed his triumph to divine assistance. He stressed, however, that if Russia reduced her military strength, disaster might overrun her as it had destroyed the empire of the Greeks.

In these final years the Tsar was preoccupied with a most difficult problem. Who would succeed him? Alexis had been sacrificed to make way for Catherine's son.

But in April, 1719, the young prince had fallen ill and died. Catherine had no other son, but one male Romanov did remain, the son of Alexis. Many rightly claimed him to be the lawful heir. Peter was not hostile to the child, but he realized that with his grandson on the throne the partisans of Alexis would most likely regain power.

In 1721, the Tsar asked the Senate and the Synod to accept Catherine as empress. Had he considered appointing her his successor? If that were so he seems to have temporarily changed his mind, for he formed a liaison with Maria Cantemir, daughter of a Moldavian prince. Maria was with child, yet the Tsar took her, as well as Catherine, with him on his Persian campaign.

These were bad moments for Catherine and Menshikov. What would Catherine's fate be if Maria bore a son? Would the child be Peter's heir? The Tsar had already published a manifesto claiming the right to decide who should succeed him. (Unfortunately for Maria, the child was born prematurely and died, and this ended Peter's interest in her.)

In December, 1722, the Tsar and Catherine journeyed to Moscow. During the victory celebrations they stayed part of the time at Preobrazhenskoye. There Peter did a rather peculiar thing; he set fire to the small house that he had himself built in his youth. As the flames roared, he walked round them banging a drum.

One would have thought that he would have wanted to preserve the house. But he explained that there he had prepared for the conquest of the Swedes; now its destruction symbolized that he had fulfilled his task.

Perhaps the burning was nothing more than an impulsive act on Peter's part. Or did he feel that his life was drawing to a close? During the early months of 1723, he must have given much thought again to the question of succession. Of the people who entered his mind, Catherine appears to have been paramount. As his consort she had shown enthusiasm for his reforms. Who else would be more likely to ensure that they continued after his death?

He made his decision in November, 1723. In a manifesto he praised Catherine, expressing his wish to crown her—"our great helper, especially in the campaign on the Prut." But apparently he was still undecided, for six months went by before the coronation.

But in May, 1724, the former Livonian peasant, amid pomp and pageantry, knelt before the Tsar in the cathedral of the Kremlin. She was resplendent in a purple gown adorned with gold and a headdress that glittered with diamonds and pearls. Peter, gay in red stockings and a pale-blue tunic embroidered in silver, took the imperial crown from the Archbishop of Novgorod and placed it on Catherine's head. He also anointed his wife, an act which scandalized many people since they interpreted it as a sign that she would be the future monarch.

>>>><<<

17

>>>>>>>>><<<<<<<<<

FROM MEDIEVALISM TO MODERNITY

Whether Peter suspected it or not, the curtain was closing on his eventful life. But he was to do one more thing which would add luster to the capital he had created in the Neva marshes. Petersburg had risen in a desolate area where, according to tradition, St. Alexander Nevsky had conquered the Swedes in 1541.

In commemoration Peter had ordered the erection of the Alexander Nevsky monastery. But now, in 1724, this was not enough: the remains of the saint must be brought to Petersburg.

The relics were borne to Novgorod, where they were placed aboard Peter's yacht and conveyed to Lake

Ladoga. Accompanied by vessels of his fleet, the Tsar, at the helm of a rowing boat, met the yacht at Ust-Izhora. There the box containing the relics was lowered into the boat for Petersburg. The Tsar helped to take it ashore, and it was carried beneath an ornate canopy to the church of St. Alexander.

From that time on, the capital would be known as St. Petersburg, a decision which was accompanied by the traditional feasting.

Peter's health had been deteriorating for some time, and the effect of this latest revelry forced him to take to his bed. Some chroniclers have implied that this drinking bout hastened his end. His sickness continued to get worse, and the once iron constitution grew weak. On September 22, 1724, the facial contortions returned: Peter had a fit. Yet he stubbornly ignored all medical advice; indeed, his doctors fled when he began to brandish his cudgel. His senior physician appealed to the Tsar to rest, but a domestic drama destroyed any chance of tranquillity.

Having raised Catherine to the rank of empress, Peter was both angry and jealous to learn that she had deceived him. Her lover was her chamberlain, William Mons, brother of Anna, the Tsar's companion of his youth. Peter, who was striving to eradicate graft, was even more furious on learning that Mons was capitalizing on his influence with Catherine. Both he and his sister Matrena had grown rich on bribes.

Had the empress profited herself? After Mons died

on the scaffold on November 14, Peter ordered an inquiry into her wealth. To prevent Catherine from further misusing her power, he decreed also that any order issued in her name was now valueless unless it also bore his signature. Characteristically, he arranged that when she retired to her bedroom, she found there Mons's head preserved in spirits.

The Tsar must have been lonelier than ever. Whom could he trust? He was aware that if Catherine succeeded him it would, in effect, endow Menshikov—whom he knew was corrupt—with total power. Wishing to undermine him, and certainly wishing to weaken the political relationship between him and Catherine, Peter replaced Menshikov with Prince Anikita Repnin as president of the War Department.

Despite his failing health, Peter was as active as ever. In October, he had surveyed the Ladoga Canal. From there he went to the Olonets ironworks, then visited the salt factory at Staraya Russa. It had been early November when he started to sail back to the capital. At Lakhty, a small town near Petersburg, the Tsar plunged into the icy water to help salvage a vessel aground in the shallows.

The incident must have taxed his weakened state. Yet some days after the death of Mons he sanctioned the betrothal of Anne, his eldest daughter, to the Duke of Holstein. Accompanied by Catherine, Peter attended the Church of the Holy Trinity and before a great assembly placed the rings on the fingers of the couple.

Utterly disregarding medical advice, the Tsar used what strength remained for drinking bouts throughout Christmas and into the New Year. It had been customary to attend the annual blessing of the waters of the Neva at the Feast of the Epiphany. That ceremony in 1725 would be his last. Fever finally sapped his strength, and he would never leave his bedroom at Mon Plaisir alive.

In his suffering, Peter's thoughts turned to God, and he asked that a chapel be consecrated outside his door. On January 22, he made his confession and received the sacrament. Four days later, close to death, Peter was anointed with oil. He pardoned all prisoners save those guilty of murder. On the following day this amnesty embraced all those condemned to death for a military offense, and nobles who had evaded army service.

During the afternoon Peter attempted to write, but the strain was too great. He got no further than the words: "Give back all to . . ." Then he asked for Anne, his daughter, intending to dictate the rest. But it was too late: he fell into a deep coma.

The empress wept at his side and the dignitaries of Church, state, army, and navy watched as their sovereign's life gradually ended.

In the early hours of January 28, 1725, Peter the Great died. As his body lay in the soft light of the ikon lamps, the question of succession was already being discussed elsewhere. Presumably Catherine met the senators, allowing them to decide her future. Soon after, Catherine was proclaimed the lawful holder of the crown.

It has been implied that the senators had no alternative. Catherine and Menshikov are said to have gained the support of the Guard. There is no doubt that if the army had disagreed with the choice, Catherine could never have ascended the throne.

But ascend she did, although Catherine I did not reign for long, and was followed by Peter's grandson, Peter II, who was the son of Alexis. After his death in 1730, a niece of Peter the Great came to the throne. In 1741, Peter's daughter Elizabeth succeeded her. Her rule lasted until 1762, when her nephew became Peter III. Because he proved unfit to rule, he was removed, and his wife came to power as Catherine II, or Catherine the Great, the first ruler of any stature since the death of Peter I. The line of the tsars continued until the early twentieth century when the reigning monarch and his family were executed. In 1917, the Communist party gained control of the country and began the social revolution which has brought about the Soviet Union as we know it today.

Peter the Great had been a tyrant, at times brutal, and he had known much violence. On the day of his funeral it seemed that nature was determined to be in keeping. Snow and hail swept down in blustering squalls as the cortege moved slowly to the cathedral in the fortress.

In his oration Prokopovich had this to say of the Tsar: ". . . This is Peter the Great whom we are committing to earth. . . . He has gone, but his work will survive him. He has left us, but he does not leave us in destitution and poverty. He made Russia powerful and so she will remain. . . ."

Without doubt, Peter the Great had been titanic in character. So were the changes that he effected in Russia. For two decades he strove to drive his nation from medievalism to modernity, from an Eastern to a Western state.

By no means did he succeed completely, but this does not detract from the immensity of his achievements. The transition had been too quick. He strenuously tilled the soil and sowed the seeds of civilization, although he knew that the plants would only thrive after his death. There lurks the radiant quality of his genius.

Before he ascended the throne, Russian sway in Europe was so slight that it could virtually be discounted. Afterward it was tremendous and could not be ignored. That, briefly, is the essence of Peter's greatness.

EVENTS IN THE LIFE OF PETER THE GREAT

1672	Born in the Kremlin on June 11
1682	Comes to the throne (shared with stepbrother Ivan); moves to Preobrazhenskoye with his mother
1689	Marries Eudoxia Lopukhin; commits the regent, his stepsister Sophia, to a convent
1691	His Preobrazhensky and Semenovsky regiments begin their great careers
1694	Founds the Russian navy at Archangel with the *Santa Profeetie*
1696	Ivan dies and Peter becomes the sole ruler; he takes Azov
1697	Peter makes his first Continental tour

1698 Punishes and disbands the streltsy

1700 Ends the office of Patriarch; introduces the new calendar; joins Poland and Denmark against Sweden; Northern War begins

1701 School of Mathematical Science and Navigation founded

1703 Foundations of Petersburg laid

1704 Capture of Dorpat and Narva

1704–5 Many new taxes imposed

1708 Victory at Lesnoy

1709 Wins the Battle of Poltava

1710 Books in Russian begin to appear; conquest of Karelia

1711 Introduces the Senate; failure of the campaign against Turkey

1712 Official marriage to Catherine

1713 Now master of a substantial strip of Baltic coast

1716 His second European tour

1718 His son Alexis renounces his claim to the throne; Alexis is executed

1721 Peace of Nystad is concluded; Peter receives his new titles; establishes the Holy Synod

1724 Crowns Catherine in Moscow; his capital renamed St. Petersburg

1725 Dies at St. Petersburg on January 28

INDEX

INDEX

INDEX